Getting Started
with
High School
Sentence
Composing

Getting Started
with
High School Sentence Composing

A Student Worktext

Don and Jenny Killgallon

HEINEMANN
Portsmouth, NH

Heinemann
145 Maplewood Ave., Suite 300
Portsmouth, NH 03801
www.heinemann.com

Offices and agents throughout the world

Library of Congress Cataloging-in-Publication Data

Names: Killgallon, Don, author. | Killgallon, Jenny, author.
Title: Getting started with high school sentence composing : a student
    worktext / Don and Jenny Killgallon.
Description: Portsmouth, NH: Heinemann, 2018. | Audience: Age 14–18. |
    Audience: Grade 9 to 12.
Identifiers: LCCN 2018003343 | ISBN 9780325098166
Subjects: LCSH: English language—Sentences—Study and teaching (Secondary) |
    English language—Composition and exercises—Study and teaching
    (Secondary) | English language—Sentences—Problems, exercises, etc.
Classification: LCC LB1631 .K467 2018 | DDC 808/.0420712—dc23

LC record available at https://lccn.loc.gov/2018003343

Acquisitions Editor: Tobey Antao
Production Editor: Sean Moreau
Cover and Interior Designs: Monica Crigler
Typesetter: Cape Cod Compositors, Inc.
Manufacturing: Steve Bernier

Printed in the United States of America on acid-free paper

2 3 4 5 6 PP 27 26 25 24 23
June 2023 Printing 4500873686

CONTENTS

This book uses an original approach to strengthen your sentences by imitating authors at their best. Their way of building sentences can improve your skill as a sentence builder. You will learn how to use their sentence-composing power tools to write more strongly and read more skillfully to be at your best.

Inside, you'll meet new words, but you'll get instant help to learn what they mean. A quickshot is a familiar word placed right next to an unfamiliar word to keep you reading without stumbling.

BASIC SENTENCE TRAINING

Before learning how to build better sentences, you need to know what a sentence is, what its parts are, and what tools good writers use to build strong sentences.

REPAIRING BROKEN SENTENCES

Sentence-composing tools are sentence parts, not complete sentences. If a tool is written with a capital letter and ends with a period, it is a broken sentence, just a piece of a sentence, a fragment. In this section you'll learn to spot and repair broken sentences, or, even better, avoid them in your writing.

LEARNING BY IMITATING   29

To learn how to do something, you imitate people who know how. In this section, you'll see how to build better sentences by imitating professional writers. In the next section, you'll use imitation to learn tools authors use to build their sentences in ways you can build your sentences.

PREVIEW: THE SENTENCE-COMPOSING POWER TOOLS   41

After this preview of the tools—**extender, identifier, describer, elaborator**—you'll learn and practice each tool to put all four power tools in your sentence-composing toolbox.

EXTENDER TOOL   44

You'll imitate and compose sentences like this:

> The sailors caught an enormous shark, thrashing on deck wickedly in its death throes, **while no one dared go near enough to club it**.
>
> —Isabel Allende, *Daughter of Fortune*

IDENTIFIER TOOL   60

You'll imitate and compose sentences like this:

> The hangman, **a gray-haired convict in the white uniform of the prison**, was waiting beside his machine.
>
> —George Orwell, "A Hanging"

DESCRIBER TOOL   76

You'll imitate and compose sentences like this:

> He was up in a moment, **pounding at the secret spring until the door popped open**.

> —Stephen King, *The Eyes of the Dragon*

ELABORATOR TOOL   94

You'll imitate and compose sentences like this:

> **My hands and limbs swollen with snake venom**, my face and bare skin had red welts.

> —Keith Donohue, *The Stolen Child*

REVIEW: THE SENTENCE-COMPOSING POWER TOOLS   111

After this review of the tools—**extender, identifier, describer, elaborator**—you'll then see how those tools are sometimes combined within the same sentence.

COMBO TOOL   114

You'll imitate and compose sentences like this:

> His paper, **a report of a herd of ten thousand dinosaurs living along the shore** (*identifier*), **building nests of eggs in the mud** (*describer*), **their infant dinosaurs raised in the herd** (*elaborator*), made Grant a celebrity overnight **after he spent years as an unknown** (*extender*).

> —Michael Crichton, *Jurassic Park*

THE TOOLBOX   126

To get the job done right in your sentences, use the right tools. You've learned the right tools: *the extender, the identifier, the describer, the elaborator, the combo.* Those power tools are in your toolbox. Now get ready to use them in this section by building strong sentences with those tools. When you finish, admire your work, done right with the right tools, and take a bow.

Nothing is more satisfying than to write a good sentence.

—Barbara Tuchman, historian

QUICKSHOTS FOR NEW WORDS

Sentences sometimes contain unfamiliar words. Take this sentence by Rudolph Giuliani, then mayor of New York City, condemning the terrorist attacks of September 11, 2001.

There's no moral way to sympathize
with grossly immoral actions.

The meaning of the sentence is roughly this: *There's no [SOMETHING] way to sympathize with grossly [SOMETHING] actions.* What way? What actions? There's no way to tell—other than that something is pretty bad. Maybe it's time for a dictionary to find out what *moral* means, and its opposite *immoral*.

Good news: In this worktext, you don't need a dictionary. Instead, a quickshot will immediately tell you the meaning of *moral* and *immoral*. Throughout this worktext when individual words are **bold** [*darkened*], a fast definition—a quickshot—will be **adjacent** [*beside it*]. If you already know the word, just keep reading. If you don't, a quickshot will keep you reading without stumbling.

With quickshots, you can skip the dictionary and keep reading, stumble-free. Now reread the sentence, this time with quickshots for *moral* and *immoral*.

----

*There's no **moral** [right] way to sympathize*
*with grossly **immoral** [wrong] actions.*

Quickshots are fast and easy, but not perfect. For example, you now know that *moral* means *right*, *immoral* means *wrong*, but only for human behavior that's right or wrong.

On a spelling test, if you got most of the words right, you wouldn't say, "I got most spellings moral, but some immoral." Spellings aren't human behavior. People behave, not words, so only people can behave morally (rightly) or immorally (wrongly).

QUICKSHOTS IN THIS WORKTEXT

If a word might be a stumbling block, there's a quickshot to help you keep reading. The quickshot unlocks the word's meaning. Knowing the word's meaning often also unlocks the meaning of the sentence.

Following is a paragraph about Esperanza, a Mexican girl age twelve who lives on a farm where grapes are grown. To honor his daughter, her father asks her to cut down the first cluster of grapes to celebrate the start of the harvest. You'll see the paragraph first without quickshots, and then with quickshots.

Description Without Quickshots

(1) Her father **extended** the knife to Esperanza. (2) The short blade was curved, its fat wooden handle fitting **snugly** in her hand. (3) This job was usually **reserved** for the **eldest** son of a wealthy rancher, but since Esperanza was an only child, she was always given the **honor**. (4) The grape **clusters** were heavy on the vine. (5) Esperanza's parents stood by, Mama, tall and **elegant**, her hair in braids, and Papa, **barely** taller than Mama, his graying mustache twisting up at the sides. (6) He pointed his hand toward the grapevines, **signaling** Esperanza. (7) When she walked toward the vines and **glanced** back at her parents, they both smiled and nodded. (8) When she reached the vines, she separated the leaves and carefully **grasped** a thick stem. (9) She put her knife to it, and with a quick **swipe**, the heavy grapes dropped into her hand to give to Papa, who kissed it, then held it up for all to see.

—Pam Muñoz Ryan, *Esperanza Rising* (adapted)

Description with Quickshots

(1) Her father **extended** [*handed*] the knife to Esperanza. (2) The short blade was curved, its fat wooden handle fitting **snugly** [*tightly*] in her hand. (3) This job was usually **reserved** [*saved*] for the **eldest** [*oldest*] son of a wealthy rancher, but since Esperanza was an only child, she was always given the **honor** [*privilege*]. (4) The grape **clusters** [*bunches*] were heavy on the vine. (5) Esperanza's parents stood by, Mama, tall and **elegant** [*beautiful*], her hair in braids, and Papa, **barely** [*hardly*] taller than Mama, his graying mustache twisting up at the sides. (6) He pointed his hand toward the grapevines, **signaling** [*directing*] Esperanza to come. (7) When she walked toward the vines and **glanced** [*looked*] back at her parents, they both smiled and nodded. (8) When she reached the vines, she separated the leaves and carefully **grasped** [*held*] a thick stem. (9) She put her knife to it, and with a quick **swipe** [*cut*], the heavy grapes dropped into her hand to give to Papa, who kissed it, then held it up for all to see.

Description with Just the Easier Words

(1) Her father handed Esperanza the knife. (2) The short blade was curved, its fat wooden handle fitting tightly in her hand. (3) This job was usually saved for the oldest son of a wealthy rancher, but since Esperanza was an only child, she was always given the privilege. (4) The grape bunches were heavy on the vine. (5) Esperanza's parents stood by, Mama, tall and beautiful, her hair in braids, and Papa, hardly taller than Mama, his graying mustache twisting up at the sides. (6) He pointed his hand toward the grapevines, directing Esperanza to come. (7) When she walked toward the vines and looked back at her parents, they both smiled and nodded. (8) When she reached the vines, she separated the leaves and carefully held a thick stem. (9) She put her knife to it, and with a quick cut, the heavy grapes dropped into her hand to give to Papa, who kissed it, then held it up for all to see.

I ran across many words whose meanings I did not know,
and I either looked them up in a dictionary or, before I
*had a chance to do that, **encountered** [met] the word in a*
__context__ [sentence] that made its meaning clear.

—Richard Wright, *Black Boy*

With quickshots, you don't need to look up new words, or struggle to figure them out.

QUIZ: QUICKSHOTS

Directions: Quickshots are very short, so they are easier than dictionary definitions to remember. See how many you remember. Match the word with its definition.

1. Bullying on the playground by pushing or punching smaller kids is **immoral**.

   a. fun   **b.** wrong   **c.** right   **d.** easy

2. After deciding not to copy Angelina's homework, Arlene was happy with her **moral** choice.

   a. unusual   **b.** right   **c.** difficult   **d.** final

3. The principal **extended** the diploma to Enrique.

   a. threw   **b.** handed   **c.** flew   **d.** tossed

4. During the blizzard, inside the house, Grandma wore a wool blanket **snugly** around her body.

   a. loosely   **b.** poorly   **c.** tightly   **d.** easily

5. As the **eldest** daughter, Janna often felt that she was given more responsibility than her sisters.

    a. smartest   **b.** strongest   **c.** oldest   **d.** nearest

6. It is an **honor** to be selected for any kind of reward or accomplishment.

    a. privilege   **b.** payment   **c.** challenge   **d.** treat

7. Cranston could **barely** touch the bottom of the basketball net.

    a. easily   **b.** amazingly   **c.** always   **d.** hardly

8. A **cluster** of flowers was planted at the entrance to our house.

    a. mixture   **b.** bunch   **c.** mound   **d.** vase

9. Many girls who were considered cute would rather be considered **elegant**.

    a. beautiful   **b.** smart   **c.** funny   **d.** holy

10. In the crowded cafeteria line, he **glanced** at the clock to see if he had enough time.

    a. stopped   **b.** stood   **c.** looked   **d.** stared

SUBJECTS AND PREDICATES

A sentence is a comment about a topic. The topic is called *a subject*. The comment about the topic is called *a predicate*. Every sentence needs both a subject and a predicate. Look at these sentences about octopuses.

SUBJECT (topic)	PREDICATE (comment about the topic)
1. All octopuses	can squeeze through tight openings impossible to other sea creatures because octopuses have no skeleton.
2. Their body parts	include two eyes, eight arms, and one hard beak used to crush the shells of crabs they eat.
3. Coral reefs	are shelters where octopuses can live safer from enemies.
4. Only one kind of octopus	can kill a human through its deadly venom.
5. Black ink that they spray	defends octopuses against attackers and allows them to move to safety.

ACTIVITY 1: MATCHING SUBJECTS AND PREDICATES

Directions: Match the subject with its predicate to make a sentence. Write out each sentence.

SUBJECTS	PREDICATES
1. Several spiders ^ *—Harry Potter and the Chamber of Secrets*	**a.** came suddenly out of the shadows.
2. The snake ^ *—Harry Potter and the Sorcerer's Stone*	**b.** were thrown onto their backs with their endless legs waving in the air.
3. A voice ^ *—Harry Potter and the Prisoner of Azkaban*	**c.** sat back down on the sofa, which **sagged** [*sank*] under his weight.

4. The giant ^ —*Harry Potter and the Sorcerer's Stone*	**d.** was about as safe as poking a sleeping dragon in the eye.
5. Misbehavior [*doing wrong*] in Snape's class ^ —*Harry Potter and the Chamber of Secrets* (adapted)	**e.** raised its head until its eyes were on a level with Harry's.

ACTIVITY 2: CREATING SUBJECTS

Directions: Write interesting subjects for these predicates to make a complete sentence. Make your subjects several words long as in the following example.

EXAMPLE

Predicate: . . . stood in a semicircle wearing red scarves round their throats.

POSSIBLE SUBJECTS

a. **A bunch of my friends at the corner for the school bus** stood in a semicircle wearing red scarves round their throats.

b. **Derek and the rest of the basketball team** stood in a semicircle wearing red scarves round their throats.

c. **The teachers at the school entrance** stood in a semicircle wearing red scarves round their throats.

Author's Sentence

Some eight or ten little field-mice stood in a semicircle wearing red scarves round their throats.

—Kenneth Grahame, *The Wind in the Willows*

1. ... made them stir but not wake.

   —Toni Morrison, *Beloved*

2. ... would just look at you and smile and show her yellow teeth.

   —Judith Ortiz Cofer, *Silent Dancing*

3. ... began **scavenging** [*searching for food*] by pulling pizzas out of the dumpster behind a pizza delivery shop.

   —Lars Eighner, "On Dumpster Diving"

4. ... burst into the room again, wearing old jeans and a torn T-shirt.

   —Maya Angelou, *The Heart of a Woman*

5. ... came in from the dry country in search of a drink, and sometimes fell into the swimming pool and found themselves trapped by walls of shiny, unclimbable tiles.

   —Wallace Stegner, *Crossing to Safety* (adapted)

ACTIVITY 3: CREATING PREDICATES

Directions: Write interesting predicates for these subjects to make complete sentences. Make your predicates several words long as in the following example.

EXAMPLE

   Subject: The faded red doors . . .

SAMPLE PREDICATES

a. were removed by the carpenter.

b. faced a large window in the restaurant.

c. needed a fresh coat of paint.

> ### *Author's Sentence*
> The faded red doors swung open.
>
> —Kate DiCamillo, *The Tiger Rising*

---

1. Big, rough teen-agers. . . .

   —Robert Lipsyte, *The Contender*

2. The baby's eyes. . . .

   —Anne Tyler, *Digging to America*

3. The factories. . . .

   —Keith Donohue, *The Stolen Child*

4. Our fist-fight at recess. . . .

   —Jon Katz, "How Boys Become Men"

5. A great many old people. . . .

   —Langston Hughes, *The Big Sea*

QUIZ: SUBJECTS AND PREDICATES

Directions: Jot down whether the statement is true or false.

1. Sometimes complete sentences contain only a subject (topic) but no predicate (comment about that topic).   T

2. Sometimes complete sentences contain only a predicate but no subject.   F

3. The following sentence contains a subject with two parts, not one.

   Dead rats and frogs started appearing in his locker about three
   months earlier.   T

   —Gary Paulsen, *The Time Hackers*

4. The following sentence contains a predicate with exactly three parts.

   An arrow squealed out of the dark, sliced a wedge from his ear,
   nicked the horse of the man riding behind him, and skittered away
   like a bat.

   —Peter S. Beagle, *The Last Unicorn*

5. All complete sentences contain both a subject, which is a topic, and a predicate, which is a comment about the topic.

MY WRITING: INFORMATIONAL SENTENCES

Pretend you are writing a pamphlet about animals in a zoo to provide visitors facts. Online or offline, find out lots of interesting information about *one* of these: lions, bears, zebras, elephants, tigers, giraffes—or some other animal.

   Then write five sentences between ten and twenty words long about your creature. Make sure each sentence has an informative subject and predicate.

SENTENCE-COMPOSING TOOLS

What makes the best hamburger? First, you'll need two basics: bread and meat. Then you'll want more: maybe cheese, catsup or mustard, onions, tomato, lettuce, pickles, and so forth. Add-ons make it tastier, and the best.

What makes the best sentence? First, you'll need two requirements: a subject and a predicate. Although those two parts are necessary, they are not the most important parts of the best sentences.

The most important parts are sentence-composing tools. They add detail to your sentences, providing information beyond the subject and predicate. Like hamburgers, add-ons also make sentences tastier, and the best.

Take a look at the following examples. The first sentence in each pair has just a subject and predicate. The second sentence has the same subject and predicate but also sentence-composing tools. Tools are bolded.

On the Mark: Tools need commas that separate them from the rest of the sentence.

EXAMPLES

1a. The snakes lay with their chins resting on their own coils.

1b. In the rattlesnake cage, the snakes lay with their chins resting on their own coils, **looking straight ahead out of their black eyes**.

—John Steinbeck, *Cannery Row* (adapted)

What the Tools Add: The first tool tells readers where the snakes were (*in the rattlesnake cage*). The tool at the end of the sentence tells what the snakes were doing (*looking straight ahead out of their black eyes*).

2a. Spectators at the huge fire responded by chopping up wooden fences and sidewalks.

2b. Spectators at the huge fire, **who were asked to help**, responded by chopping up wooden fences and sidewalks, **hoping to deprive the fire of fuel**. (*Contains two tools.*)

—Jim Murphy, *The Great Fire*

What the Tools Add: The first tool tells readers what the spectators were asked to do (*who were asked to help*). The tool at the end of the sentence tells why the spectators were chopping up things (*hoping to deprive the fire of fuel*).

3a. The earthen floor and the path get flooded and muddy and wet for several days.

3b. **When it rains**, the earthen floor and the path get flooded and muddy and wet for several days, **giving off a smell that reminds you of rotting fish**. (*Contains two tools.*)

—Richard Kim, *Lost Names*

What the Tools Add: The first tool tells readers when the event happens (*when it rains*). The tool at the end of the sentence tells what odor results from the flooding (*giving off a smell that reminds you of rotting fish*).

4a. Kiser Pease was creating clouds of dust.

4b. **In the distance**, Kiser Pease, **on his tractor**, was creating clouds of dust.

—Bill and Vera Cleaver, *Where the Lilies Bloom*

What the Tools Add: The first tool tells readers where the event happens (*in the distance*). The tool in the middle of the sentence tells where Kiser was (*on his tractor*).

5a. He arrived home each day filthy.

5b. Although each night Big Ma prepared a pot of hot soapy water for him to wash out his clothing, he arrived home each day filthy, **looking as if his pants had not been washed in more than a month**.

—Mildred D. Taylor, *Roll of Thunder, Hear My Cry*

What the Tools Add: The first tool tells readers how the mother tried to help her son (*although each night Big Ma prepared a pot of hot soapy water for him to wash out his clothing*). The tool at the end of the sentence tells that his pants got dirty anyway (*looking as if his pants had not been washed in more than a month*).

ACTIVITY 1: IDENTIFYING SENTENCE PARTS

Directions: Jot down the letter for the kind of sentence part.

>   *S* for subject
>
>   *P* for predicate
>
>   *T* for tool

Note: There is a subject (S) and a predicate (P) in each list. The other sentence parts are tools (T).

EXAMPLE (*Commas separate tools from the rest of the sentence.*)

a. Although he became famous playing baseball,

b. Jackie Robinson

c. preferred football and starred on UCLA's team.

—Barry Denenberg, *Stealing Home*

ANSWERS

a. T

b. S

c. P

PART ONE

These sentences contain a subject and a predicate and just one tool.

1a. I

1b. loved school with a desperate passion,

1c. which became more intense when I began to realize what a **monumental** [*big*] struggle it was for my parents and brothers and sisters to keep me there.

> —Eugenia Collier, "Sweet Potato Pie"

2a. Trying to look like the ball players he had seen the time his father had taken him to the Polo Ground,

2b. Marty

2c. ran into the outfield and took the position near the curb

> —Murray Heyert, "The New Kid" (adapted)

3a. When black powder is too dry or mixed in the wrong formula,

3b. almost anything

3c. can set it off without warning.

> —John Fleischman, *Phineas Gage*

4a. Mama

4b. offered Mr. Morrison Grandpa Logan's chair,

4c. a cushioned oak rocker skillfully crafted by Grandpa himself

   —Mildred D. Taylor, *Roll of Thunder, Hear My Cry*

5a. Sandy and Dennis,

5b. the ten-year-old twin brothers who got home from school an hour earlier than she did,

5c. were disgusted.

   —Madeleine L'Engle, *A Wrinkle in Time*

PART TWO

These sentences contain a subject, a predicate, and more than one tool.

6a. Suddenly,

6b. Gollum

6c. sat down and began to weep,

6d. a whistling and **gurgling** [*bubbling*] sound horrible to listen to.

   —J. R. R. Tolkien, *The Hobbit*

7a. When the thirteen colonies were first settled,

7b. most immigrants

7c. came from England, Holland, and France,

7d. followed soon afterwards by Scandinavians, Welsh, Scots, Scot-Irish, Irish, and Germans.

   —Ellen Levine, *If Your Name Was Changed at Ellis Island*

8a. Luckily,

8b. Leo,

8c. the snow leopard cub,

8d. was rescued by a kind goatherd and his family,

8e. who hand-fed Leo and kept him safe.

—Craig and Isabella Hatkoff, *Leo the Snow Leopard*

9a. Sometimes,

9b. the dinosaurs

9c. reared up on their **hind** [*back*] legs,

9d. resting their forelegs on the tree trunks

9e. so that they could reach the leaves on higher branches.

—Michael Crichton, *Jurassic Park*

10a. In my opinion,

10b. a truly great quarterback

10c. plays at a very high level on the field and off the field as well,

10d. a guy who plays like a champion,

10e. not only on Sundays but also on every other day of the week.

—Mark Brunell and Drew Brees, *Coming Back Stronger*

Question: What two sentence parts cannot be removed without destroying the sentence? What sentence parts can be removed without destroying the sentence?

Answer: The subject and the predicate cannot be removed because if you take out either, the sentence is destroyed. Tools can be removed, but good writers don't remove them because they add information and tastiness to sentences.

SENTENCE-COMPOSING TOOL FACTS

A tool is a sentence part that adds detail to a sentence.

1. Tools can be placed in the *beginning*, *middle*, or *end* of a sentence.	They can appear in the beginning, with a *comma after the tool*.
	When one of its arms is missing because of an accident or attack, an octopus can quickly grow a replacement.
	They can appear in the middle, with a *comma before and after the tool*.
	The octopus with the longest life, **the giant Pacific octopus,** doesn't live long enough after the young are born to teach them very much.
	They can appear at the end with a *comma before the tool*.
	An octopus has three hearts, **two of which pump blood into its gills and one of which pumps blood into the rest of its body.**
2. A tool can be a *word*.	**Amazingly,** a female octopus lays 20,000 to 100,000 eggs.
3. A tool can be a *phrase*. A phrase is a group of words without a subject and predicate.	Octopuses, **dependent on their need for salt water,** live only in oceans.
4. A tool can be a *dependent clause*. A dependent clause is a sentence part containing a subject and predicate, but it is not a sentence, only a part of a sentence.	**After the male octopus mates,** he dies.

5. Sentences can have several tools, together or apart.	Tools Together **Equipped with a sense of smell, housed in the sensors at the end of their arms**, octopuses by inserting an arm into a crevice detect what might be lurking there. Tools Apart **At the end of its arms,** an octopus has suction cups, **which allow it to taste food, accepting or rejecting the food according to whether it likes the taste.**
6. Tools can be short, medium, or long.	Short **To protect itself**, an octopus ejects a thick black cloud to hide in and then escape. Medium Octopuses also use camouflage for protection, **produced by skin cells that can change the skin's apparent color**. Long **Injecting poison into the shellfish to dissolve the shell to make eating the soft tissue possible**, an octopus can get to and eat the food.

QUIZ: SENTENCE-COMPOSING TOOLS

Directions: Jot down whether the statement is true or false.

1. Tools are complete sentences.

2. Tools can be placed at the beginning or end of a sentence but not in the middle of a sentence.

3. This sentence contains exactly three tools.

    > About a year after the incident, Tommy talked to a former gang member named Felix, a young man he'd known as a baby.
    >
    > —Tracy Kidder, *Home Town*

4. The following sentence contains a subject and a predicate but no tools.

    > Daring not to glance at the books, I went out of the library, fearing that the librarian would call me back for further questioning.
    >
    > —Richard Wright, *Black Boy*

5. In the following sentence, the sentence part with the fewest words is the subject:

    > The young Italian, who had called to her earlier in the evening and who was now apparently setting out on his own Sunday evening's adventures, came along the sidewalk and walked quickly away into the darkness.
    >
    > —Sherwood Anderson, "Unlighted Lamps"

MY WRITING: INFORMATIONAL SENTENCES

Find out more information about some other fascinating animal. Then write five sentences between ten and twenty words long about your animal. In each sentence, be sure to include a subject and predicate and one or more sentence-composing tools.

REVIEW

- For subjects and predicates, reread the five sentences about octopuses on page 6.

- For sentence-composing tools, reread more sentences about octopuses on pages 17–18.

FRAGMENTS

A fragment is a big problem. A fragment looks like a sentence because it has a capital letter at the beginning and a period at the end, but it is not a sentence. It is a broken sentence, only a sentence part, just a fragment of a complete sentence.

EXAMPLES

1a. *Complete Sentence:* When he lived in the city, he had a lot of friends.
—Lorenz Graham, "Hitchhiker"

1b. *Fragment:* When he lived in the city.

2a. *Complete Sentence:* A man stood in the doorway, his suit as black as oil.
—Rick Riordan, *A Maze of Bones*

2b. *Fragment:* His suit as black as oil.

3a. *Complete Sentence:* Muscles flexing tightly against his thin shirt, he lifted the truck in one powerful motion until the front was off the ground.
—Mildred D. Taylor, *Roll of Thunder, Hear My Cry*

3b. *Fragment:* Muscles flexing tightly against his thin shirt.

4a. *Complete Sentence:* Because the eyes of the china rabbit were painted on and he could not close them, he was always awake.
—Kate DiCamillo, *The Miraculous Journey of Edward Tulane*

4b. *Fragment:* Because the eyes of the china rabbit were painted on and he could not close them.

5a. *Complete Sentence:* Mr. Murry, who had been sitting, rose.
—Madeleine L'Engle, *A Wrinkle in Time* (adapted)

5b. *Fragment:* Who had been sitting.

Plates accidentally broken into fragments can be repaired; so can sentences broken into fragments. In this section, you will learn how to fix broken sentences, or—even better—avoid them completely.

ACTIVITY 1: SPOTTING AND GLUING FRAGMENTS

Directions: Each group has a sentence and two fragments. Tell which is the sentence and which are the two fragments. Then glue the fragments back into the sentence at the beginning or the end—whichever makes more sense.

On the Mark: When you glue fragments into sentences, commas are needed.

EXAMPLE

a. When she finished crying. (*fragment*)

b. She wiped her face with the palms of her hands. (*sentence*)

c. Feeling no better but out of tears. (*fragment*)

Good Arrangements

When she finished crying, she wiped her face with the palms of her hands, feeling no better but out of tears. (*One is glued at the beginning of the sentence, and one at the end of the sentence.*)

OR

When she finished crying, feeling no better but out of tears, she wiped her face with the palms of her hands. (*Both are glued at the beginning of the sentence.*)

—Lynne Reid Banks, *One More River*

1a. He stared in amazement at a small purple hole in it.

1b. Moving his arm only a little.

1c. Halfway between his wrist and his elbow.

—Robb White, *Deathwatch*

2a. To make him **docile** [*obedient*].

2b. They would have done an operation on his brain.

2c. To stop him being **rebellious** [*disobedient*].

—John Christopher, *The Guardians*

3a. Shielding the lenses of their flashlights.

3b. The boys began a thorough search of the wooded section.

3c. So that the light beams would not be easily **detected** [*seen*] by anyone **lurking** [*hiding*] in the **vicinity** [*area*].

—Franklin W. Dixon, *The Secret of the Old Mill*

4a. Its front two clutching him tightly below a pair of shining black **pincers** [*claws*].

4b. Harry saw that what had hold of him was marching on six long, hairy legs.

4c. His head hanging below.

—J. K. Rowling, *Harry Potter and the Chamber of Secrets*

5a. He didn't have any real enemies unless you counted the entire football team.

5b. Who seemed to think he was some kind of toy and were constantly playing catch with him.

5c. Throwing him up in the air or stuffing him into containers.

—Gary Paulsen, *The Time Hackers*

ACTIVITY 2: GLUING BROKEN SENTENCES BACK TOGETHER

Directions: The following paragraph, about how the Egyptian pharaoh King Tut died at age nineteen, has fragments that make reading bumpy. Glue each fragment to the sentence where it belongs—the sentence before the fragment, or the one following the fragment, whichever makes more sense. When you finish, you will have *twelve* complete sentences and no fragments. Then, reading will be smooth, not bumpy.

On the Mark: When you glue fragments into sentences, commas are needed.

Mysterious Death of Young Egyptian Pharaoh

(1) Although much has been learned about the ancient pharaoh of Egypt called King Tut. (2) One mystery remains. (3) Despite many **theories** [*ideas*] about how the pharaoh died. (4) No one is actually sure. (5) The theories include that he was murdered by enemies, that he died of an infection. (6) And that he was crushed by a hippopotamus. (7) Backed up by forensic x-rays and explanations. (8) The newest theory suggests that he was run over by a chariot. (9) Using special equipment to solve crimes. (10) The crime lab examined all of the evidence to create a **virtual** [*realistic*] **autopsy** [*a study of the cause of death*]. (11) Revealing that King Tut's body on his left side is missing eight ribs. (12) Plus part of his pelvis. (13) Usually left inside a mummy. (14) The heart was also missing. (15) To **simulate** [*recreate*] the accident as it might have happened. (16) The scientists used a chariot made for the movies. (17) After talking about what types of objects could cause this kind of damage. (18) Experts think the most likely object is a chariot wheel. (19) They collected **data** [*information*] on how the chariot moved at top speed. (20) Passing their findings on to specialists who create different computer **simulations** [*recreations*]. (21) The first simulation showed King Tut falling off his chariot, and the second

showed him crashing the chariot, but neither simulation matched King Tut's injuries. (22) The final simulation showed him on his knees as he fell under the wheel of an oncoming chariot. (23) Even though the injuries line up in that simulation. (24) No one is ready to close the case.

ACTIVITY 3: SOLVING A FRAGMENT PUZZLE

Directions: The following paragraph, about a dangerous trip into unexplored land along the Amazon River in South America, has to be put back together. Underneath the paragraph are broken sentences (fragments) that are parts of sentences in the original paragraph. While copying the paragraph, glue each fragment to the sentence where it belongs.
Hint: The fragments are listed after the paragraph in the order they occur in the original paragraph.

On the Mark: When you glue a fragment into a sentence, use a comma.

Attack of Piranha

Note: A piranha is a deadly South American fish with sharp teeth.

(1) Their suffering began in full force. (2) They had exhausted all their food. (3) The rivers were filled with piranha, which the men could eat, but the piranha sliced through the men's fishing line and hooks. (4) Out of desperation one man finally threw dynamite into a pond with the deadly fish. (5) He made the mistake of holding a piranha in his mouth while his hands were busy scooping up others. (6) It attacked. (7) The piranha took a bite out of his tongue. (8) He would have bled to death had the doctor not stopped the bleeding with moss.

—Candice Millard, *The River of Doubt* (adapted)

FRAGMENTS

Note: A capitalized fragment begins a sentence in the paragraph. Other fragments end a sentence in the paragraph.

a. As the men hacked their way through the deepening jungle

b. By late August

c. using their knife-blade teeth

d. So difficult were piranhas to catch

e. As he splashed through the water to gather dead piranhas

f. At first stunned by the dynamite and motionless between the man's teeth

g. as soon as the piranha recovered

h. Before the man had time to react

ACTIVITY 4: REPAIRING BROKEN SENTENCES

Directions: Make the fragment a part of a complete sentence.

EXAMPLE

Fragment: because the weather was unbearably hot

SAMPLE REPAIRS

a. Because the weather was unbearably hot, **Tamara stopped jogging and walked the rest of the way back to the dorm**.

b. **The corn in the field started to wilt** because the weather was unbearably hot.

Directions: Make the fragment into a sentence part *at the beginning* of a complete sentence.

1. *Fragment:* When our school's winning team appeared.

    Sample Repair: When our school's winning team appeared, the fans yelled and cheered for the champion.

2. *Fragment:* To decide if it was worth the price.

    Sample Repair: To decide if it was worth the price, I did as much research as I could on the Internet and by talking to friends.

3. *Fragment:* Early in the misty morning as we approached the car.

    Sample Repair: Early in the misty morning as we approached the car, we saw a cat with kittens in the back seat.

4. *Fragment:* Warning the class about the cruelty of bullying.

    Sample Repair: Warning the class about the cruelty of bullying, our teacher gave us examples from when he was in high school.

5. *Fragment:* Sometimes veering off the road while driving.

    Sample Repair: Sometimes veering off the road while driving, the student driver was told by the teacher to pay more attention.

Directions: Make the fragment into a sentence part *at the end* of a complete sentence.

6. *Fragment:* One of the most terrifying experiences I've ever had.

    Sample Repair: I once mistook the sound of a car backfiring for a gunshot, one of the most terrifying experiences I've ever had.

7. *Fragment:* Resulting in almost losing a finger.

    Sample Repair: When I first began woodworking in class, I didn't know what I was doing, resulting in almost losing a finger.

8. *Fragment:* Which teachers forbid during class.

   Sample Repair: In the back of the classroom some kids were secretly playing with their phones, which teachers forbid during class.

9. *Fragment:* A slug slimier than the eel in biology class.

   Sample Repair: When we were barefoot in the mud, my right foot felt something, a slug slimier than the eel in biology class.

10. *Fragment:* Signaling smoke from the burned pie in the oven.

    Sample Repair: The smoke detector sounded, signaling smoke from the burned pie in the oven.

QUIZ: FRAGMENTS

Directions: Jot down whether the statement is true or false.

1. Fragments are always sentence parts instead of complete sentences.

2. Fragments cannot be repaired.

3. Putting a capital letter at the beginning of a fragment and a period at its end sometimes repairs a fragment.

4. Fragments can always be joined to the sentence that comes before them, but never to the sentence that comes after them.

5. The following paragraph contains two fragments.

   Gilly **obligingly** [*obediently*] took the gum out of her mouth. While Miss Ellis's eyes were still in the rearview mirror. When the social worker turned her attention back to the traffic, Gilly carefully spread the gum under the handle of the car door. As a sticky surprise for the next person who might try to open it.

   —Katherine Paterson, *The Great Gilly Hopkins*

LEARNING BY IMITATING

"Please show me how to do that." You've probably asked people to show you how to do something: swing a bat, style your hair, drive a car, make a recipe, solve a math problem—just about anything.

Those activities, and many more, show that imitating is a good way to learn. Throughout this worktext, you'll see how authors build their sentences, imitate how they do it, and then build your sentences like they do.

First, look at some sentence imitations. Following is a model with five imitations of that model. All six sentences—the model and the imitations—mean something different, but they all have the same kinds of sentence parts. In other words, the imitations are built like the model.

> *Model Sentence:* Earth, the little blue and green planet, the one with the fluffy white clouds and all, is under attack.
> —K. A. Applegate, *Animorphs: The Underground*

IMITATION SENTENCES

1. Chickenpox, the highly contagious and airborne disease, the one with the itchy red rash and blisters, is never pleasant.

2. *Titanic*, the incredibly luxurious but sinking ship, the boat with the very hopeful passengers and crew, was certainly doomed.

3. The brain, the supremely important and necessary organ, the center of the entire human body and mind, is always important.

4. Auroras, the beautifully colorful and memorable displays, the lights with a lovely reddish tint and green, are often dazzling.

5. Venom, the highly feared and poisonous saliva, the substance in some poisonous deadly reptiles and insects, is sometimes fatal.

WHAT MAKES A GOOD MODEL SENTENCE?

Sentences worth imitating appear in almost everything we read. Throughout this worktext are hundreds of model sentences from all kinds of writing, from classics like *To Kill a Mockingbird*, from fantasies like the Harry Potter novels, from popular favorites like *The Hunger Games*, from children's literature like *A Wrinkle in Time*, and from spy stories, horror stories, true stories, love stories, sports stories, funny stories, sci-fi stories, and on and on.

Despite the wide range of sources—from children's literature to classic novels, all the model sentences in *Getting Started with High School Sentence Composing* illustrate the use of powerful tools to build powerful sentences.

Those tools are the focus of this worktext. After learning them through the activities in this worktext, you, too, can be a builder of powerful sentences. Here are a few samples.

1. **When he was nearly thirteen**, my brother Jem got his arm badly broken at the elbow.

    —Harper Lee, *To Kill a Mockingbird*

2. Every year, Harry was left behind with Mrs. Figg, **a mad old lady who lived two streets away**.

    —J. K. Rowling, *Harry Potter and the Sorcerer's Stone*

3. The pain hit me suddenly, **racking my body with sobs**.

    —Suzanne Collins, *The Hunger Games*

4. A blond little boy looked very small sitting there alone in the big old-fashioned kitchen, **his feet swinging a good six inches above the floor**.

    —Madeleine L'Engle, *A Wrinkle in Time*

The powerful tools in those four sentences are examples of the sentence-building tools you'll learn, practice, and use through the activities in this worktext, then use to build your own powerful sentences in and beyond high school.

ACTIVITY 1: UNDERSTANDING SENTENCE PARTS

Directions: To imitate a sentence, first you need to see its parts. In reading and writing, understanding sentence parts is necessary. Read the following sentences broken into meaningful sentence parts. Pause after each slash mark.

EXAMPLES

1. Clare snored, / quiet animal snores / that felt like bulldozers / running through my head.
    —Audrey Niffenegger, *The Time Traveler's Wife*

2. It was nearly dark outside now, / and the rain was still coming down, / pattering against the windows / and blurring the lights / of the cars / in the street outside.
    —Neil Gaiman, *Coraline*

3. On a Saturday afternoon / in July 1938, / a half-starved teenager / wandered into a bus station / in Columbus, Ohio, / appearing confused and disoriented.
    —Laura Hillenbrand, *Seabiscuit*

4. Emilio stood in the hospital morgue / to identify his wife and child, / a doctor of medicine lifting off a sheet / and exposing their faces, / their eyes closed, / their expressions surprisingly **serene** [*calm*].
    —Oscar Hijuelos, *The Fourteen Sisters of Emilio Montez O'Brien*

5. The baseball struck my mother's left temple, / spinning her so quickly that one of her high heels broke / and she fell forward, / her knees splaying apart, / her face hitting the ground first / because her hands / never moved from her sides, / killing her / before she touched the ground.

> —John Irving, *A Prayer for Owen Meany*

ACTIVITY 2: SPOTTING IMITATION SENTENCES

Directions: Underneath the author's sentence are three sentences. Which *two* sentences imitate the author's sentence because, although different in meaning, they are alike in structure?

1. *Model Sentence:* Inside his office, he napped for an hour, snoring so loudly that his secretary finally had to close his door.

   > —John Grisham, *The Brethren*

   a. At her desk, she studied for the test, concentrating so intensely that her roommate eventually had to leave the room.

   b. The children by the river played contentedly, making odd dolls dressed in colorful leaves from the tree above them.

   c. Across the field, she ran like a gazelle, moving so gracefully that her coach ultimately decided to choose her.

2. *Model Sentence:* Threading his way through the Ninsei crowds, he could smell his own stale sweat.

   > —William Gibson, *Neuromancer*

   a. Walking slowly through the departing crowd emphasized their disappointment with the outcome.

b. Tapping the rhythm to the complicated song, he would imagine his own original variation

c. Dancing her part in the Broadway musical, she could picture her own rising star.

3. *Model Sentence:* She flicked her magic wand casually at the dishes in the sink, which began to clean themselves, clinking gently in the background.

   —J. K. Rowling, *Harry Potter and the Chamber of Secrets*

   a. Alonso tossed his muddy shirt suddenly at the children in the pool, who wanted to play around, laughing together at the silliness.

   b. The fairy flapped her lovely wings quietly over the castle near the lake, which started to resemble a mirror, reflecting magically in the moonlight.

   c. Selma noticed a suspicious person in the news conference and wondered why he was there taking notes and asking questions.

4. *Model Sentence:* They recalled the chicken salad Leroy brought to the Labor Day picnic, which had been sitting in the rear window of his car for a few hours, and the waves of propulsive vomiting it caused.

   —Garrison Keillor, *Pontoon*

   a. No one had prepared them for the intensity of the storm, and for the danger that they were sailing into, the possibility of a tornado hitting the lake and the surrounding area.

   b. The students discussed the unreasonable demands Matilda brought to the student council monthly meeting, which had been festering in the back of her mind since the last meeting, and the outburst of unanticipated anger those demands released.

c. They noticed the outrageous, flamboyant costume Henry wore to the high school Halloween dance, which had been stored in the dank garage of his neighbor for a few years, and the jeers of cruel laughter it evoked.

5. *Model Sentence:* In the mango grove, shade poured into his black eyes when he played as a boy, when his mother sang, when the sacred offerings were made, when his father taught him, when the wise men talked.

—Hermann Hesse, *Siddhartha*

a. In the school room, colors danced across the blank walls as he fantasized in his imagination, as the teacher smiled, as the quirky music was played, as his friend tickled him, as the other children giggled.

b. Under the large tree where he had played as a child he often thought about the people he would no longer see, the places he would no longer go, the times that were no more, remembering the past warmly and with longing.

c. On the playing field, energy surged throughout his agile body, when he kicked like a pro, when his coach applauded, when the ritual exercises were completed, when his teammates applauded him, when the loyal fans cheered.

ACTIVITY 3: MATCHING MODEL AND IMITATION SENTENCES

Directions: Match the imitation with the model it imitates.

Model Sentence	Imitation Sentence
1. On the floor, his scarred, bony head resting on one of the man's feet, lay an old white English bull terrier. —Sheila Burnford, *The Incredible Journey*	**a.** They did love the fragrant jasmine plant, its scent lifting gently onto the breeze, floating effortlessly in the air a few moments ago.
2. She always blamed him for bringing her all the way from Alabama to Michigan, a state she called a giant icebox. —Christopher Paul Curtis, *The Watsons Go to Birmingham—1963*	**b.** We are now experiencing artificial intelligence, the wave of the certain future, a world of technology now appearing in many applications.
3. Kit could see the little wooden doll, its arms sticking stiffly into the air, bobbing helplessly in the water a few feet away. —Elizabeth George Speare, *The Witch of Blackbird Pond*	**c.** In the night, their flickering, flashing signals lighting up all of the dark landscape, appeared a large energetic firefly insect swarm.
4. You are now entering Jurassic Park, the world of the prehistoric past, a world of creatures long gone from the earth. —Michael Crichton, *Jurassic Park*	**d.** A child in a pink blouse, a sobbing sound coming from her little voice, dropped her ice cream on the sidewalk.
5. A teenager in a black tank top, a greenish tattoo flowing across her broad back, hoisted a toddler onto her shoulder. —Barbara Kingsolver, *Animal Dreams*	**e.** Jolene deeply thanked him for helping her in the years from childhood to adolescence, a time she cried a large river.

ACTIVITY 4: UNSCRAMBLING TO IMITATE

Directions: Unscramble the sentence parts to imitate the model sentence. Start with the first sentence part listed.

On the Mark: Put commas the same places as in the model sentence.

EXAMPLE

Model Sentence: Propped on her elbows with her chin in her fists, she stared at the black wolf, trying to catch his eye.

—Jean Craighead George, *Julie of the Wolves*

SENTENCE PARTS TO UNSCRAMBLE TO IMITATE THE MODEL SENTENCE

a. (*Start here.*) Sitting in his car with his phone in his hand

b. hoping to beat the crowd

c. Dante

d. looked at the GPS directions

Imitation Sentence: Sitting in his car with his phone in his hand, Dante looked at the GPS directions, hoping to beat the crowd.

---

1. *Model Sentence:* Troubled, he limped carefully around the snake.
    —Alexander Key, *The Forgotten Door*

    a. (*Start here.*) Confused

    b. at the problem

    c. stared blindly

    d. Maybelle

2. *Model Sentence:* In the winter, when everything's frozen, I hate the mountains.

 —Bill and Vera Cleaver, *Where the Lilies Bloom*

 a. (*Start here.*) On our porch

 b. love the summer

 c. we

 d. where furniture's cozy

3. *Model Sentence:* In the starlight, her eyes saw an owl, two rabbits, a striped cat from town, a jay sleeping on a branch.

 —Hal Borland, *When the Legends Die*

 a. (*Start here.*) From the suitcase

 b. a new pair of jeans

 c. her hands pulled out a blouse

 d. a coat hung on a hanger

 e. some jewelry

4. *Model Sentence:* About midnight, huddled shivering under his blankets in the darkness, he began to wonder if he should give up and go home.

 —Thomas Rockwell, *How to Eat Fried Worms*

 a. (*Start here.*) At camp

 b. Danny tried to decide

 c. whether he should remain still

 d. awakened wondering about the noise outside his tent

 e. or go outside

5. *Model Sentence:* Overwhelmed by pain, Jonas lay there in the **stench** [*odor*] for hours, listened to the men and animals die, and learned what warfare meant.

—Lois Lowry, The Giver

a. (*Start here.*) Outsmarted by the opposition

b. and understood what mistake happened

c. heard the quarterback and coach talk

d. on the sidelines for advice

e. Henry waited there

ACTIVITY 5: IMITATING MODEL SENTENCES

Directions: Study the model sentence and a sample imitation of the model sentence to see how both sentences are built alike. Then write your own imitation about something you know, something you've experienced, or something you've seen in the media.

> **Tip:** Take it easy. Imitate one sentence part at a time. Here are the sentence parts of the model and its imitation.

Model Sentence Parts	Imitation Sentence Parts
1. a. The poplar trees	**a.** The curious toddler
b. lined the redbrick driveway,	**b.** touched the stuffed animal,
c. which led to a pair of wrought-iron gates. —Khaled Hosseini, *The Kite Runner*	**c.** which felt like a blanket of soft furry velvet.

2. a. McTeague remembered his mother, **b.** who, with the help **c.** of an assistant, **d.** cooked for forty miners. —Frank Norris, *McTeague* (adapted)	**a.** Frankie watched the pitcher, **b.** who, with the concentration **c.** of a surgeon, **d.** hurled his best fast ball.
3. a. This boy was an **ingenious** [*clever*] liar, **b.** a lonely boy **c.** with a boundless desire **d.** to ingratiate himself. —Marilynne Robinson, *Housekeeping*	**a.** That dog was a dangerous pet **b.** a vicious dog **c.** with a distinct tendency **d.** to bite anyone.
4. a. He lived alone, **b.** a **gaunt** [*thin*], stooped figure **c.** who wore a heavy black overcoat **d.** and a misshapen hat on those rare occasions **e.** when he left his apartment. —Barack Obama, *Dreams from My Father*	**a.** She worked hard, **b.** an ambitious, outspoken manager **c.** who wanted an impressive job title **d.** and a corner office on the top floor **e.** before she turned thirty.
5. a. After the clerk stamped the envelope, **b.** and threw it into a sorting bin, **c.** I sat down, **d.** **glum** [*depressed*], **e.** and disheartened. —Yann Martel, *Life of Pi*	**a.** When the others heard the call **b.** and answered it with a shrill scream, **c.** I felt alone, **d.** sad, **e.** and abandoned.

Learning to build strong sentences by imitating the way authors build strong sentences makes sense because it works.

In the next section, you'll see four sentence-composing power tools authors use to build their strong sentences. Then, in the rest of this worktext, you'll learn, practice, and use those four tools to build your sentences the way authors build theirs.

PREVIEW: THE SENTENCE-COMPOSING POWER TOOLS

In the sentence-composing toolbox of good writers are four power tools: *the extender*, *the identifier*, *the describer*, and *the elaborator*. They provide four ways to build better sentences like those of famous authors.

The tools can be anywhere in a sentence: the beginning, the middle, or the end.

EXTENDER TOOLS enlarge meaning within a sentence.

1. When he was nearly thirteen, my brother Jem got his arm badly broken at the elbow.

    —Harper Lee, *To Kill a Mockingbird*

2. A huge dog, as we passed an open doorway, came bounding out, snarling and barking at us.

    —Peter Abrahams, *Tell Freedom*

3. No **hobgoblin** [*monster*] appeared, although a black cat did try to cross my path.

    —Keith Donohue, *The Stolen Child*

IDENTIFIER TOOLS identify someone or something.

4. The thin and olive-skinned boys, Ragno and Zanzara each had a thatch of dark curls on his head and was quick to anger and quicker to forgive.

    —Keith Donohue, *The Stolen Child*

5. In the late afternoon, Will Henderson, the owner and editor of the *Eagle* newspaper, went over to Tom Willy's **saloon** [*bar*].

    —Sherwood Anderson, *Winesburg, Ohio*

6. In her wallet she still carried a picture of her husband, <u>a clean-shaven boy in his twenties with hair parted on one side.</u>

> —Jhumpa Lahiri, *Unaccustomed Earth*

DESCRIBER TOOLS describe someone or something.

7. <u>Hissing furiously</u>, the snake **slithered** [*crawled*] straight toward Justin and raised itself again with its fangs exposed and **poised** [*ready*] to strike.

> —J. K. Rowling, *Harry Potter and the Chamber of Secrets* (adapted)

8. Al grinned, <u>revealing his missing teeth and unhealthy gums.</u>

> —Stephen King, *11/22/63*

9. A big kitchen table was neatly set as if for a big party, <u>covered with one of those old-fashioned oilcloths.</u>

> —Robert Cormier, *Take Me Where the Good Times Are* (adapted)

ELABORATOR TOOLS add details for full understanding.

10. <u>His blood pooling red on the black asphalt</u>, then, slowly, he fell to his knees and pitched forward onto the road.

> —Robert Ludlum, *The Moscow Vector* (adapted)

11. The dead man's face, <u>his eyes wide open and teeth **bared** [*visible*] and grinning with an expression of **unendurable** [*horrible*] agony,</u> was coated with mud.

> —George Orwell, "Shooting an Elephant"

12. Sometimes I feel about eight years old, <u>my body squeezed up and everything else tall</u>.

> —Ray Bradbury, *The Martian Chronicles*

Coming up are the most important activities in this worktext because they will help you learn, practice, imitate, and compose strong sentences built with those four sentence-composing power tools.

After carefully doing those activities, you can build your sentences like those of real authors, who use those same powerful sentence-composing tools all the time.

You'll never get anywhere with all those
damn little short sentences.

—Gregory Clark, *A Social Perspective on the Function of Writing*

EXTENDER TOOL

Extenders (adverb clauses) are sentence parts that enlarge meaning within a sentence. Most extenders begin with one of these words: *after*, *although*, *as*, *because*, *before*, *if*, *since*, *until*, *when*, *while*.

An extender is like a sentence within a sentence because the extender has a subject and predicate just like a sentence. The first word of an extender makes it a sentence part that links the extender to the rest of the sentence.

Warning: If an extender is written like a sentence, it is a fragment problem, not a sentence.

1. SENTENCE: Sophie's mother was in a bad mood.

2. FRAGMENT: When Sophie's mother was in a bad mood.

3. EXTENDER: **When Sophie's mother was in a bad mood**, she would call the house they lived in a zoo.

   —Jostein Gaarder, *Sophie's World*

Read the following sentence pairs. The extenders are **bolded**, and what they extend is underlined. These sentences show how extenders build better sentences.

1a. He quit the vocational school.

1b. When he was sixteen, he quit the vocational school. (*Extender is in the beginning.*)

   —Bernard Malamud, "The Prison" (adapted)

2a. The first floor was where the rats lived.

2b. The first floor, **because it was closest to the garbage in the empty lot**, was where the rats lived. (*Extender is in the middle.*)

—Walter Dean Myers, *Motown and Didi*

3a. His feet slipped out from under him.

3b. His feet slipped out from under him **as he raced through a pile of dead leaves**. (*Extender is at the end.*)

—Robert Ludlum, *The Moscow Vector*

ACTIVITY 1: MATCHING

Directions: Insert the extender into the sentence at the caret (^). To practice using the extender tool, copy and punctuate the sentence.

Sentence	Extender
1. ^ , we were let out into the playground twice a day for a short recess and at lunchtime. —Keith Donohue, *The Stolen Child*	**a.** as the dragon charged
2. ^ , everybody for a hundred yards snapped their heads around at the sound. —Michael Crichton, *Travels*	**b.** because a hungry tarantula will pay no attention to a loudly chirping cricket placed in its cage
3. ^ , most Californians were young Americans who had families back east. —Stephen E. Ambrose, *Nothing Like It in the World*	**c.** although they came from different ports and different continents and by different routes
4. ^ , it released huge clouds of hissing steam through its nostrils. —Heywood Broun, "The Fifty-First Dragon"	**d.** when the snake wrangler pulled out the plywood boxes with snakes out of the station wagon

5. Tarantulas apparently have little or no sense of hearing, ^ . —Alexander Petrunkevitch, "The Spider and the Wasp"	**e.** if the weather cooperated

ACTIVITY 2: EXCHANGING

Directions: Replace the extender with one of yours that fits the rest of the sentence. Make your extender about the same length as the author's extender. Begin your extender with the same word as the author's extender. The extenders are **bolded**, and what they extend is underlined.

EXAMPLE

Author's Extender

His feet slipped out from under him **as he raced through a pile of dead leaves**.

—Robert Ludlum, *The Moscow Vector*

Your Extender

His feet slipped out from under him **as he hit a patch of unexpected ice**. (*Many other extenders are possible.*)

----

1. **When it rained**, her hair curled all over the back of her neck. (*In your extender, tell another time her hair curled up. Begin with* When.)

   —Stephen Vincent Benet, "Too Early Spring"

2. **Because he was so small**, Stuart was often hard to find around the house. (*In your extender, tell another reason Stuart was hard to find. Begin with* Because.)

   —Keith Donohue, *The Stolen Child*

3. The girls were still sleeping, **although they had changed positions while she was gone**. (*In your extender, tell what other things they might have done while asleep. Begin with* although.)

   —Toni Morrison, *Beloved*

4. **Before I could protest,** they disappeared and faded into the forest like ghostly wolves. (*In your extender, tell what else might have happened before they disappeared. Begin with* Before.)

   —Keith Donohue, *The Stolen Child* (adapted)

5. The thunder and lightning were frightening **while the rain came in gusts and torrents**. (*In your extender, tell what else might have happened during the storm. Begin with* while.)

   —Kate Shelly, "Iowa Heroine"

ACTIVITY 3: UNSCRAMBLING

Directions: Unscramble the sentence parts to imitate the model sentence. Start with the first sentence part listed. Write out the imitation sentence and underline the extender.

On the Mark: Put commas the same places as in the model sentence.

EXAMPLE

> *Model Sentence:* If you asked her a question, she would just look at you and smile, showing her yellow teeth.
> —Judith Ortiz Cofer, *Silent Dancing*

SENTENCE PARTS TO UNSCRAMBLE TO IMITATE THE MODEL SENTENCE

a. (*Start here.*) If someone gave you a million dollars

b. thanking your lucky stars

c. and stutter

d. you would probably stare at that person

> *Imitation Sentence:* If someone gave you a million dollars, you would probably stare at that person and stutter, thanking your lucky stars.

---

1. *Model Sentence:* Then she reached down, picked the boy up by his shirt front, and shook him until his teeth rattled.
   —Langston Hughes, "Thank You, M'am"

   a. (*Start here.*) Suddenly the tornado touched down

   b. until the buildings crumbled

   c. and battered it

   d. entered the town near its town center

2. *Model Sentence:* The tiny dragon awkwardly explored the room and squealed as it bumped into a wall or furniture.
   —Christopher Paolini, *Eragon* (adapted)

   a. (*Start here.*) The water snake

   b. as it touched a rock or fish

   c. and jerked

   d. slowly entered the stream

3. *Model Sentence:* Sawyer shouted at her when she entered the kitchen, but she just turned her back and reached for her apron.
   —Toni Morrison, *Beloved*

   a. (*Start here.*) Mrs. Santosa scowled at Carlos

   b. but he just took his seat

c. and opened up his book

d. when he entered the classroom

4.   In the night, while Captain Tinker was asleep, Jenny the cat came downstairs and searched the downstairs closets.
   —Esther Averill, *Jenny and the Cat Club*

a. (*Start here.*) During the storm

b. and hated the sudden thunderclaps

c. Peas the dog

d. while his owners were away

e. shivered upstairs

5.   The very next morning, before anyone else was awake, Podhu took a spear, slung a skin bag over one shoulder, and leaving the house, walked to the forest.
   —Humphrey Hartmen, "Podhu and Aruwa"

a. (*Start here.)* The nearly last moment

b. and taking the reins, galloped to the battle

c. the general loaded his gun

d. mounted a black stallion with quick skill

e. before battle troops had arrived

ACTIVITY 4: COMBINING

Directions: Combine the **bold** parts into just one sentence that imitates the model. Write the imitation sentence and underline any extender tools. You'll learn that several weak sentences can be combined into just one strong sentence.

On the Mark: Put commas the same places as in the model sentence.

EXAMPLE

Model Sentence: President Roosevelt, although only two years older than Truman, seemed a tired old man.

—David McCullough, *Truman*

SENTENCES TO COMBINE INTO JUST ONE SENTENCE

a. This is about **the Hope Diamond**.

b. It was in a museum **although it was only a small exhibit in the museum**.

c. The Hope Diamond **attracted** something.

d. It attracted **a huge curious crowd**.

Resulting Sentence: The Hope Diamond, <u>although it was only a small exhibit in the museum</u>, attracted a huge curious crowd.

---

1. ***Model Sentence:*** The canyon, if you strip it down, is a great, granite bowl of air.

   —Barbara Kingsolver, *Animal Dreams*

   a. Here is a comment about **your smile**.

   b. That smile, **if you give it away**, is something.

   c. It **is a warm, wonderful gift**.

   d. It is a gift **of joy**.

2. *Model Sentence:* He beat the creature off with his hands until he remembered his sword and drew it out.

—J. R. R. Tolkien, *The Hobbit* (adapted)

a. Edwin settled the children down.

b. He settled them down **with his voice**.

c. He did this **until he calmed their shouting**.

d. And he did this until he **quieted them down**.

3. *Model Sentence:* While he was sitting with her on the side of the bed, Mary came to the door and said that the missus wanted to see him in the parlor.

—James Joyce, "The Boarding House"

a. Something happened **while Mom was preparing for the party**.

b. The preparing was **at the table on the deck**.

c. Dad went to the neighbors and said something to them.

d. He said **that their children needed to** do something.

e. What they needed to do was to **join them for the party**.

4. *Model Sentence:* He was running fast now, narrowly dodging tree trunks and low-hanging branches as they loomed up suddenly in front of him.

—Robert Ludlum, *The Moscow Vector* (adapted)

a. He was swimming hard then.

b. He was **frequently hitting flood debris**.

c. And he was constantly hitting **dead fish**.

d. As they floated by grotesquely, he was touching them.

e. They floated by **in water around him**.

5. *Model Sentence:* It was dark when I got up in the morning and frosty when I followed my breath to school. (*Contains two extenders.*)

—Julia Alvarez, "Snow"

a. **I was happy** when something happened.

b. **When I did well on a test** I was happy.

c. **And** I was **disappointed** when the opposite happened.

d. The disappointment was **when I failed a test**.

e. The disappointment happened **in school**.

ACTIVITY 5: IMITATING

Directions: The model sentence and sample imitation contain extenders and are built alike. Write an imitation sentence about something you know, something you've experienced, or something you've seen in the media. Read the model sentence, then its imitation, then your imitation. If all three are built pretty much alike, congratulations!

> **Tip:** Take it easy. Imitate one sentence part at a time. Here are the sentence parts of the model and its imitation.

Model Sentence Parts	Imitation Sentence Parts
1. a. As Beson turned during the fight,	**a.** As Alexandra walked toward the stove,
b. he was rocked	**b.** she was aware
c. by left hooks and right jabs. —Stephen King, *The Eyes of the Dragon*	**c.** of wonderful aromas and appetizing sights.

2. a. That night in Max's room **b.** a forest **c.** grew and grew and grew **d.** until his ceiling hung with vines. —Maurice Sendak, *Where the Wild Things Are*	**a.** That moment in Lita's mind **b.** a thought **c.** turned and turned and turned **d.** until the idea buzzed with energy.
3. a. When Harry opened the door, **b.** Fang shot off through the trees **c.** to Hagrid's house, **d.** his tail between his legs. —J. K. Rowling, *Harry Potter and the Chamber of Secrets* (adapted)	**a.** After Nate finished the Lego, **b.** he straightened up around his room **c.** in their apartment, **d.** his hands with his toys.
4. a. As he walked, **b.** he saw a movement on the ground, **c.** and saw a rat **d.** take its head from a paper bag **e.** and **regard** [*watch*] him. —John Cheever, "The Five-Forty-Eight"	**a.** As Ben strained, **b.** he got a cramp in his hand, **c.** and felt a pain **d.** move its way into his numbing arm **e.** and disable him.
5. a. When she grinned, **b.** her baby teeth shone **c.** like a string of pearls, **d.** and when she laughed, **e.** her thin shoulders shook. —Keith Donohue, *The Stolen Child*	**a.** When Johnson laughed, **b.** his strong guffaw sounded **c.** like an explosion of fireworks, **d.** and when he stopped, **e.** his whole body stilled.

ACTIVITY 6: EXPANDING

Directions: The extender has been removed from the author's sentence. At the caret (^), create an extender **several words long** that blends with the rest of the sentence. Most extenders begin with one of these words: *after, although, as, because, before, if, since, until, when, while.*

EXAMPLE

Extender Removed

The captain stopped the motor **before** ^ . (*In several words, tell what happened before the captain stopped the motor.*)

Your Extender

The captain stopped the motor **before the ship collided with an iceberg**. (*Many other extenders are possible.*)

Author's Extender

The captain stopped the motor **before they reached the island.**
        —James Kruss, "Mr. Singer's Nicknames"

----

1. He could only see the thing's eyes, but he could feel its hairy legs **as** ^ . (*In several words, tell what he could feel the thing doing to him.*)
        —J. R. R. Tolkien, *The Hobbit*

2. **If** ^ , she took off like a bat, dancing in circles. (*In several words, tell what made her move that way.*)
        —Keith Donohue, *The Stolen Child* (adapted)

3. **When** ^ , the boy's mother would wrap the leftover biscuits in a clean flour sack and put them away for the next meal. (*In several words, tell when she would do this with the leftover biscuits.*)
        —William H. Armstrong, *Sounder*

4. **Before** ^ , Thomas bloodied their noses and backed them into a corner, pounding their faces. (*In several words, tell what was about to happen before Thomas beat them.*)

   —Hal Borland, *When the Legends Die* (adapted)

5. She dropped her books on the sidewalk **while** ^ . (*In several words, tell what happened while she dropped her books.*)

   —Toni Cade Bambara, "Geraldine Moore the Poet"

ACTIVITY 7: MULTIPLYING

Directions: The original sentence contained more than one extender. At the carets (^), create extenders **several words long** that blend with the rest of the sentence. Most extenders begin with one of these words: *after, although, as, because, before, if, since, until, when, while.*

EXAMPLE

Extenders Removed
When ^, she was kept out of the way, and **when** ^ , she was kept out of the way also.

Your Extenders
When Sally was throwing a tantrum, she was kept out of the way, and **when she was mean to her little brother**, she was kept out of the way also. (*Many other extenders are possible.*)

Author's Extenders

When she was a sickly, fretful, ugly little baby, she was kept out of the way, and **when she became a sickly, fretful, toddling thing**, she was kept out of the way also.

—Frances Hodgson Burnett, *The Secret Garden*

----

1. **If** ^ , you are cute, and **if** ^ , you are smart,
    —Betsy Byars, *The Summer of the Swans*

2. **As** ^ , I saw the bear stand on its hind feet like a man **while** ^ .
    —Fred Gipson, *Old Yeller* (adapted)

3. **When** ^ , the truck drivers simply left their trucks in the middle of the streets **until** ^ .
    —Jean Merrill, *The Pushcart War*

4. **As** ^ , Ferdinand grew and grew **until** ^ .
    —Munro Leaf, "The Story of Ferdinand"

5. **Because** ^ , **because** ^ , **because** ^ , I thought things would be different.
    —James Howe, *Addie on the Inside*

QUIZ: EXTENDERS

Directions: Jot down whether the statement is true or false.

1. This sentence has two extenders.

   She must have just climbed out of the water, because she was still dripping and because her hair was plastered against her cheeks.
   —Stephen King, *Bag of Bones*

2. The extender is the longest part of this sentence:

   The car must have flipped over on its side, because he was lying on his back against the passenger door and looking up at the steering wheel and beyond at the branches of a tree moving in the wind.
   —Michael Crichton, *Jurassic Park*

3. This sentence contains no extender tools:

   As the last gong of the bell **reverberated** [*sounded*] across the compound, I swooped up my pencils and notebook and ran inside.
   —Mildred D. Taylor, *Roll of Thunder, Hear My Cry*

4. This is a fragment problem, not an extender tool, because it is not connected to a sentence.

   Although they were uncomfortably wet.
   —Franklin W. Dixon, *The Hardy Boys: The Secret of the Old Mill*

5. Both underlined sentence parts are extender tools.

   When Mom and a friend drove up, Dad and some of his buddies were on a cliff of the canyon, trying to work up the nerve to dive into the lake forty feet below.
   —Jeannette Walls, *The Glass Castle*

MY WRITING: EXTENDER TOOLS

Now it's your turn to use the extender tool to build your own terrific sentences. You've learned that this tool is great for enlarging meaning within a sentence.

Directions: Write six sentences about either famous people or famous places, or a mixture of both. The only must-have is a detailed extender in each sentence. Remember to begin your extenders with one of these words: *after*, *although*, *as*, *because*, *before*, *if*, *since*, *until*, *when*, *while*.

   Here are examples, with some extenders at the beginning of the sentence, some in the middle, some at the end. Place your extenders in any of those places.

Beginning Extender	Subject	Predicate
Famous Person **When he was a newly elected president in 2009,**	Barack Obama	was awarded the Nobel Peace Prize in 2009 for his efforts to improve international relations.
Famous Place **Since it was designed to surpass Disneyland in California,**	Disney World in Florida	contains twenty-seven themed resort hotels, four theme parks, two water parks, several golf courses, and a camping resort.

Subject	Middle Extender	Predicate
Famous Person Muhammad Ali,	**because he was the most famous and renowned boxer of all time,**	appeared on the cover of *Sports Illustrated* thirty-seven times.
Famous Place One World Trade Center,	**after an architect named David Childs was hired to design and build it,**	was erected on the site of the twin towers destroyed in terrorist attacks on September 11, 2001.

Subject	Predicate	End Extender
Famous Person The amazingly popular Harry Potter novels	earned multimillions of dollars for first-time novelist J. K. Rowling,	**because those stories appealed to readers of all ages everywhere.**
Famous Place Times Square in New York City	attracts millions of tourists annually	**since the area is one the world's greatest entertainment venues.**

IDENTIFIER TOOL

Identifiers (appositives) are sentence parts that identify people, places, or things by telling who or what they are. Most identifiers begin with one of these words: *a*, *an*, *the*. Identifiers can appear in a sentence at the beginning, middle, or end.

Read the following sentence pairs. The identifiers are **bolded**, and what they identify is underlined. These sentences show how identifiers build better sentences.

1a. He was unprepared for the post of Navy secretary.

1b. A civilian appointee who had no experience at sea, he was unprepared for the post of Navy secretary. (*Identifier is at beginning.*)
   —Hampton Sides, *In the Kingdom of Ice*

2a. The neighbor's dog came into the house uninvited and unannounced and lifted his leg on the dining-room table.

2b. The neighbor's dog, **a male boxer inexplicably** [*strangely*] **named Rosie**, came into the house uninvited and unannounced and lifted his leg on the dining-room table. (*Identifier is in the middle.*)
   —Kate DiCamilo, *The Miraculous Journey of Edward Tulane*

3a. The dictionary had a picture of an aardvark.

3b. The dictionary had a picture of an aardvark, **a burrowing African mammal living off termites caught by sticking out its tongue as an anteater does for ants.** (*Identifier is at the end.*)
   —Malcolm X and Alex Haley, *The Autobiography of Malcolm X*

ACTIVITY 1: MATCHING

Directions: Insert the identifier into the sentence at the caret (^). To practice using the identifier tool, copy and punctuate the sentence.

Sentence	Identifier
1. My best friend was trying really hard to be sympathetic to me, ^ . —Jason Reynolds, *The Boy in the Black Suit*	**a.** a big man who had fought in Panama and during the Gulf War
2. ^ , I was put in a special seat in the first row by the window, apart from the other children so that Sister Zoe could tutor me without disturbing them. —Julia Alvarez, *How the Garcia Girls Lost Their Accents*	**b.** a pretty normal but really sad homeboy
3. In our **clenched** [*tight*] fists, we held our working cards from the shop, ^ . —Gerda Weissmann Klein, "All but My Life"	**c.** an indoor ball bat
4. Sergeant Fales, ^ , felt anger with the pain. —Mark Bowden, *Black Hawk Down*	**d.** the valuable cards that we thought meant security
5. Suddenly, Alfred, who had heard the fight from across the street, attacked from the rear with his favorite weapon, ^ . —Robert Lipsyte, *The Contender*	**e.** the only immigrant in my class

ACTIVITY 2: EXCHANGING

Directions: Replace the identifier with one of yours that fits the rest of the sentence. Make your identifier about the same length as the author's identifier. Begin your identifier with one of these words: *a*, *an*, *the*. The identifiers are **bolded**, and what they identify is underlined.

EXAMPLE

Author's Identifier
A great many old people came and knelt around us, **the women and men with rough hands**.
   —Langston Hughes, *The Big Sea*

Your Identifier
A great many old people came and knelt around us, **the retirees and grandparents with extra time**. (*Many other identifiers are possible.*)

1. Charley, **the supply manager**, came on schedule. (*Identify Charley in a new way.*)
   —Hal Borland, *When the Legends Die*

2. **A small man,** he wore a cotton shirt and a long, bloodstained smock. (*Identify the man in a new way.*)
   —Christopher Paolini, *Eragon*

3. Until a few months ago, I was a boarding student at Yancy Academy, **a private school for troubled kids in upstate New York**. (*Identify the school in a new way.*)
   —Rick Riordan, *The Lightning Thief*

4. When we got to the group home, Lester handed my file and my group-home clothes to <u>the counselor</u>, **a surfer-looking white guy named Jaden**. (*Identify Jaden in a new way.*)
—Matt de la Peña, *We Were Here*

5. There were many who came to the United States as <u>peaceful immigrants</u>, **the farmers looking for honest work and a new home as they brought their way of life from their old countries**. (*Identify the peaceful immigrants in a new way.*)
—Melvyn Bragg, *The Adventure of English* (adapted)

ACTIVITY 3: UNSCRAMBLING

Directions: Unscramble the sentence parts to imitate the model sentence. Start with the first sentence part listed. Write out the imitation sentence and <u>underline</u> the identifier.

On the Mark: Put commas the same places as in the model sentence.

EXAMPLE

Model Sentence: A veteran bronco rider, Tom Black has ridden nine horses to death in the rodeo **arena** [*ring*], and at every performance the spectators expect him to kill another one.
—Hal Borland, *When the Legends Die*

SENTENCE PARTS TO UNSCRAMBLE TO IMITATE THE MODEL SENTENCE

a. (*Start here.*) A record-breaking pilot

b. and on one attempt he broke the sound barrier to set a new record

c. had piloted many planes for experiments

d. with high-speed flying

e. Chuck Yeager

> *Imitation Sentence:* <u>A record-breaking pilot</u>, Chuck Yeager had piloted many planes for experiments with high-speed flying, and on one attempt he broke the sound barrier to set a new record.

------

1. *Model Sentence:* Argus Filch, the caretaker, was **loathed** [*hated*] by every student in the school.

   —J. K. Rowling, *Harry Potter and the Chamber of Secrets*

   a. (*Start here.*) July Fourth

   b. by most citizens of the country

   c. the birthday of the United States

   d. is celebrated

2. *Model Sentence:* The owner, a little gray man with a messy mustache and watery eyes, leaned on the counter, reading a newspaper.

   —John Steinbeck, *The Grapes of Wrath*

   a. (*Start here.*) The model

   b. walked down the runway

   c. with a bright smile and white teeth

   d. a tall lovely blonde

   e. wearing a gown

3. ***Model Sentence:*** I remember stupid stuff, the feel of a lump of oatmeal stuck on the roof of my mouth or the taste of toothpaste not rinsed off my teeth.

   —Sharon Draper, *Out of My Mind* (adapted)

   a. (*Start here.*) Alexandra remembered lovely images

   b. bright on the wall of her bedroom

   c. still stored in her memory

   d. the glow of a ray of sunshine

   e. or the appearance of rainbows

4. ***Model Sentence:*** The country hailed Althea Gibson, the tall, slim tennis player who was the first black female to win the U.S. Women's Singles.

   —Maya Angelou, *The Heart of a Woman*

   a. (*Start here.*) The Oscars honored *Star Wars*

   b. to illustrate

   c. the ongoing, popular film series

   d. that is the long interstellar story

   e. the good against evil struggle

5. ***Model Sentence:*** He had a surprisingly strong speaking voice for so small a man, an instrument he used like a sword when he addressed large crowds.

   —Daniel James Brown, *The Boys in the Boat* (adapted)

   a. (*Start here.*) The cobra

   b. when it finds unsuspecting prey

   c. has a dangerously sudden striking fang

   d. for so large a snake

   e. a weapon it uses like a killer

ACTIVITY 4: COMBINING

Directions: Combine the **bold** parts into just one sentence that imitates the model. Write the imitation sentence and underline any identifier tools. You'll learn that several weak sentences can be combined into just one strong sentence.

On the Mark: Put commas the same places as in the model sentence.

EXAMPLE

Model Sentence: I thought I'd find an easy job, <u>the kind other kids had</u>, working in the dime store or maybe a hotdog stand. (*Identifier tool is underlined.*)
> —Sandra Cisneros, *The House on Mango Street*

a. **My instructor** thought something.

b. That instructor **thought I'd become a construction engineer.**

c. Becoming a construction engineer was **the career most students wanted.**

d. As a construction engineer, I'd be **working on some big bridges.**

e. **Or perhaps** I'd be working on **some tall buildings.**

Resulting Sentence: My instructor thought I'd become a construction engineer, <u>the career most students wanted</u>, working on some big bridges or perhaps some tall buildings. (*Identifier tool is underlined.*)

1. *Model Sentence:* His target, <u>a small doe with a **pronounced** [*obvious*] limp in her left forefoot</u>, was still with the herd.
> —Christopher Paolini, *Eragon*

   a. Here is a description of **Muhammad Ali's style.**

   b. His style was **an unusual mix of a dancer's grace.**

c. The mix was **with a heavyweight punch**.

d. His style **was unmatched in the ring**.

2. *Model Sentence:* They smelled the odor of the dead goat, a garbage stench [*odor*] of decay that drifted up the hillside toward them.

  —Michael Crichton, *Jurassic Park* (adapted)

  a. This is information about **Apollo 11**.

  b. It **landed the capsule**.

  c. The landing was **on the moon's surface**.

  d. The moon's surface was **a pockmarked horizon of nothingness**.

  e. It was something **that opened up the exploration of space**.

3. *Model Sentence:* The sun hadn't quite set when we drove into Jalalabad, the capital of the state of Nangarhar famous for its fruit and warm climate.

  —Khaled Hosseini, *The Kite Runner* (adapted)

  a. This is about **our school**.

  b. It **was so excited**.

  c. The excitement was **before the field trip traveled to New York City**.

  d. That city is **the destination of many tourists of the world**.

  e. New York City is **known for its diversity and entertainment choices**.

4. *Model Sentence:* On the night of my engagement, the evening Peeta fell to his knees and **proclaimed** [*spoke*] his undying love for me in front of the cameras in the Capitol, was the night the uprising began.

  —Suzanne Collins, *Catching Fire*

  a. This is a description **at the time of the invasion**.

  b. It is about **the day the soldiers landed**.

c. The landing was **on the beaches of Normandy**.

d. The soldiers landed **and sacrificed their young lives in battle**.

e. This sacrifice was **on the world stage of World War II in Europe**.

f. The day **was the date the allies attacked**.

5. *Model Sentence:* A graduate of the United States Naval Academy with red hair and fair skin, he had a mustache that drooped over the corners of his mouth.

> —Hampton Sides, *In the Kingdom of Ice*

a. This man was **an author of the nonfiction book *Profiles in Courage***.

b. He was a man **with Irish heritage**.

c. He had that heritage **and heroic war record**.

d. His name was **John Kennedy**.

e. Kennedy **had a presidency that ended**.

f. It ended **with the tragedy of his assassination**.

ACTIVITY 5: IMITATING

Directions: The model sentence and sample imitation contain identifiers and are built alike. Write an imitation sentence about something you know, something you've experienced, or something you've seen in the media. Read the model sentence, then its imitation, then your imitation. If all three are built pretty much alike, congratulations!

> **Tip:** Take it easy. Imitate one sentence part at a time because the best way to eat an elephant is one bite at a time. Here are the sentence parts of the model and its imitation.

Model Sentence Parts	Imitation Sentence Parts
1. a. He walked right into the punch,	**a.** She stepped quickly into the water,
b. a ton of concrete	**b.** a pool of aqua
c. that slammed into his mouth. —Robert Lipsyte, *The Contender*	**c.** that concealed within its depths.
2. a. After my mother died,	**a.** When his imprisonment ended,
b. my father,	**b.** Nelson Mandela,
c. a traveling man,	**c.** a beloved leader,
d. sent me to live with his cousins. —Truman Capote, *The Grass Harp*	**d.** united his country to govern with new style.
3. a. It had a black spot on it,	**a.** The device had a strange voice within it,
b. the black spot Mr. Summers had made the night before	**b.** the strange voice artificial intelligence had designed a month ago
c. with a heavy pencil	**c.** through an expert programmer
d. in the company office. —Shirley Jackson, "The Lottery"	**d.** in the software division.
4. a. A sensationally fast runner,	**a.** An incredibly smart student,
b. Jordan had seen nothing	**b.** Einstein had experienced rejection
c. but Jesse Owens's back at the 1936 Olympic trials	**c.** and his teachers' disapproval in the various science classrooms
d. and was aiming for gold	**d.** and was hoping for recognition
e. in the Tokyo Olympics. —Laura Hillenbrand, *Unbroken*	**e.** of his remarkable theories.

5. a. A golden female moth,	**a.** A green garter snake,
b. a big one with two-inch wingspread,	**b.** a quick one with six-inch length,
c. flapped in the fire of the candle,	**c.** slid toward the foot of the tree,
d. dropped its **abdomen** [*stomach*] into the wet wax,	**d.** parted grass in the backyard,
e. stuck, flamed, and **frazzled** [*disappeared*] in a second.	**e.** stopped, sensed, and vanished in a flash.
—Annie Dillard, "Death of a Moth"	

ACTIVITY 6: EXPANDING

Directions: The identifier has been removed from the author's sentence. At the caret (^), create an identifier **several words long** that blends with the rest of the sentence.

EXAMPLE

Identifier Removed

A ^ , Thompson was a clumsy, humorless man of seventy with white hair, bug eyes, and a huge nose like a bear. (*In several words, identify Thompson.*)

Your Identifier

A really lovable guy despite his looks and personality, Thompson was a clumsy, humorless man of seventy with white hair, bug eyes, and a huge nose like a bear. (*Many other identifiers are possible.*)

Author's Identifier

A country lawyer and politician from Indiana, Thompson was a clumsy, humorless man of seventy with white hair, bug eyes, and a huge nose like a bear.

　　　　　—Hampton Sides, *In the Kingdom of Ice*

----

1. The only other person in the room, **a ^** , came over to Jelly, with his hand outstretched. (*In several words, identify the other person.*)

　　　　　—Robert Lypsyte, *The Contender*

2. It was a strange time and a mysterious journey to Jody, **an ^** . (*In several words, identify the mysterious journey.*)

　　　　　—John Steinbeck, *The Red Pony*

3. I looked out across the destroyed fields and saw Romey, **the ^** , moving around in Roy Luther's garden. (*In several words, identify Romey.*)

　　　　　—Bill and Vera Cleaver, *Where the Lilies Bloom*

4. At the man's heels trotted a dog, **a ^** . (*In several words, identify the dog.*)

　　　　　—Jack London, "To Build a Fire"

5. My mother, **a ^** , came from a large family and had many things against her. (*In several words, identify the mother.*)

　　　　　—Dr. Ben Carson, *Gifted Hands*

ACTIVITY 7: MULTIPLYING

Directions: The original sentence contained two or more identifiers. At the carets (^), create identifiers **several words long** that blend with the rest of the sentence. Most identifiers begin with one of these words: *a, an,* or *the*.

EXAMPLE

Identifiers Removed
One of them, ^ , ^, talked continually.

Your Identifiers
One of them, **a sophomore who bragged a lot, the class clown,** talked continually. (*Many other identifiers are possible.*)

Author's Identifiers
One of them, **a slender young man with white hands, the son of a jeweler in Winesburg,** talked continually.
—Sherwood Anderson, *Winesburg, Ohio*

---

1. Our father would bring presents, ^ , ^ .
   —Beverly Cleary, *Ramona and Her Father*

2. The preacher told us what we already knew about Martin Luther King, ^ and ^ .
   —Maya Angelou, *The Heart of a Woman*

3. You are now entering Jurassic Park, ^ , ^ .
   —Michael Crichton, *Jurassic Park*

4. ^ , Ned now seemed to become part of the background, ^ .
   —Erik Larson, *The Devil in the White City*

5. The amusement park had the usual attractions, ^ , ^ , ^ , and ^ .

   —Mitch Albom, *The Five People You Meet in Heaven*

QUIZ: IDENTIFIERS

Directions: Jot down whether the statement is true or false.

1. Identifiers are complete sentences.

2. Most identifiers begin with one of these words: *a, an, the*.

3. This sentence contains three identifiers telling who Hodges is.

   Hodges, the schoolmaster, came over, a round, gentle man, the most comfortable-looking man I've ever known.

   —Leslie Morris, "Three Shots for Charlie Beston"

4. The identifier is the shortest part of this sentence:

   She saw him at thirteen, a big boy with soft, dark hair, inquiring eyes, and a sensitive mouth.

   —Jessamyn West, *Cress Delahanty*

5. The worst place for the identifier is at the end of the sentence because it is not clear what is being identified.

   A founder of the American Geographical Society, Grinnell had the most extensive collection of Arctic books, maps, and charts in America.

   Grinnell, **a founder of the American Geographical Society**, had the most extensive collection of Arctic books, maps, and charts in America.

   Grinnel had the most extensive collection of Arctic books, maps, and charts in America, **a founder of the American Geographical Society**.

   —Hampton Sides, *In the Kingdom of Ice*

MY WRITING: IDENTIFIER TOOLS

Now it's your turn to use the identifier tool to build your own terrific sentences. You've learned that this tool is great for identifying people, places, or things.

Directions: Write six sentences about either famous people or famous places, or a mixture of both. The only must-have is a detailed identifier in each sentence. Remember to begin your identifiers with one of these words: *a*, *an*, *the*.

Here are examples, with some identifiers at the *beginning* of the sentence, some in the *middle*, some at the *end*. Place your identifiers in any of those places beside what the identifier is identifying.

Beginning Identifier	Subject	Predicate
Famous Person **The first African-American president of the United States of America,**	Barack Obama	was awarded the Nobel Peace Prize in 2009 for his efforts to improve international relations.
Famous Place **The most visited vacation resort in the world with an estimated fifty-two million visitors annually,**	Disney World in Florida	contains twenty-seven themed resort hotels, four theme parks, two water parks, several golf courses, and a camping resort.

Subject	Middle Identifier	Predicate
Famous Person Muhammad Ali,	**the only boxer to win the heavyweight champion-ship three times,**	appeared on the cover of *Sports Illustrated* thirty-seven times.
Famous Place One World Trade Center,	**the tallest building in the Western hemisphere at 1,776 feet,**	was erected on the site of the twin towers destroyed in terrorist attacks on September 11, 2001.

Subject	Predicate	End Identifier
Famous Person The amazingly popular Harry Potter novels	earned multimillions of dollars for first-time novelist J. K. Rowling,	**an English author whose fantasy series has sold over 500 million copies worldwide in over seventy languages.**
Famous Place Times Square in New York City	attracts millions of tourists annually,	**the gathering place every December 31 for crowds to welcome the new year when the clock strikes midnight.**

DESCRIBER TOOL

Describers (participles) are sentence parts that picture people, places, or things. Most describers begin with a word ending in *-ing* or *-ed*. Describers can appear in a sentence at the beginning, middle, or end.

   Read the following sentence pairs. The describers are **bolded**, and what they describe is <u>underlined</u>. These sentences show how describers build better sentences.

1a. The <u>soldier</u> was wet, cold, and very hungry.

1b. Lying on the floor of the car with the guns beside him under the canvas, <u>the soldier</u> was wet, cold, and very hungry. (*Describer is at the beginning.*)
>   —Ernest Hemingway, *A Farewell to Arms*

2a. The powerful <u>auto industry</u> was suddenly forced to listen for a change.

2b. The powerful <u>auto industry</u>, **accustomed to telling customers what sort of car they wanted**, was suddenly forced to listen for a change. (*Describer is in the middle.*)
>   —Jessica Mitford, *The American Way of Death*

3a. Then she trailed her fingers through the flour.

3b. Then <u>she</u> trailed her fingers through the flour, **looking for mites**. (*Describer is at the end.*)
>   —Toni Morrison, *Beloved*

Important to Remember: Describers are sentence parts that begin with words ending in *-ing* or *-ed*. Some verbs, though, also have words ending in *-ing* or *-ed*.

Tip: Here's an easy way to tell the difference. Describers have commas. Verbs don't.

EXAMPLES

Comma before the describer: From the landing the women scattered toward their homes, **hurrying before the white-edged tide that would soon cover the lower paths.**
—Kim Yong Ik, *The Sea Girl*

Comma after the describer: **Holding a hand before her eyes so that other patients and visitors should not see,** she began to weep.
—J. M. Coetzee, *Life and Times of Michael K*

Commas before and after the describer: His black hair, **plastered in place with some sort of hair potion Alan could smell,** shone in the light.
—Stephen King, *Needful Things*

TELLING THE DIFFERENCE

In each pair, tell which sentence contains a describer.

1a. The turkeys, **roosting in the tree away from coyotes**, clicked drowsily.

1b. The turkeys were **roosting in the tree away from coyotes** and clicked drowsily.
—John Steinbeck, *The Red Pony*

2a. Billy gulped down the worm, **untroubled**.

2b. Billy was **untroubled when he gulped down the worm**.
                    —Thomas Rockwell, *How to Eat Fried Worms*

3a. Huddled under my blankets, I observed the changing day.

3b. I was **huddled under my blankets** and observed the changing day.
                    —Keith Donohue, *The Stolen Child*

4a. Her eyes were filled with tears, **watching me chew the apple**.

4b. Her eyes were filled with tears while she was **watching me chew the apple**.
                    —Richard E. Kim, *Lost Names*

5a. Warmed by the unicorn's breath, the boy's fingers began to lose their stiffness.

5b. The boy's fingers were **warmed by the unicorn's breath**.
                    —Madeleine L'Engle, *A Swiftly Tilting Planet*

ACTIVITY 1: MATCHING

Directions: Insert the describer into the sentence at the caret (^). To practice using the describer tool, copy and punctuate the sentence.

Sentence	Describer
1. ^ , Harry drank the potion down in two large gulps. —J. K. Rowling, *Harry Potter and the Chamber of Secrets*	**a.** touching the leaves of the trees as I flew by
2. The family doctor, ^ , attended to him for several weeks. —Hampton Sides, *In the Kingdom of Ice*	**b. studded** [*filled*] with tears, hugs, and lipsticked kisses

3. I dreamed I was flying over a sandy beach in the early morning, ^ . —Toni Cade Bambara, "Raymond's Run"	**c.** pinching his nose
4. Our reunion with Mother in California was a joyous festival, ^ . —Maya Angelou, *The Heart of a Woman*	**d.** killing him instantly
5. The wind tore one cousin's wooden cabin clear out of the ground, threw him from the living room into his garden, and the cabin landed on top of him, ^ . —Rebecca Skloot, *The Immortal Life of Henrietta Lacks* (adapted)	**e.** worried that George might lose his hearing

ACTIVITY 2: EXCHANGING

Directions: Replace the describer with one of yours that fits the rest of the sentence. Make your describer about the same length as the author's describer. Begin your describer with a word ending in *-ing* or *-ed*. The describers are **bolded**, and what they describe is underlined.

EXAMPLE

Author's Describer

Slowly, magnificently, <u>the ship</u> rose out of the water, **gleaming in the moonlight**. (*Describe the ship in a new way beginning with an -ing describer.*)
  —J. K. Rowling, *Harry Potter and the Goblet of Fire*

Your Describer

Slowly, magnificently, <u>the ship</u> rose out of the water, **flying magically through the brilliant blue sky**. (*Many other describers are possible.*)

1. <u>Courtney</u> grabbed my hand, and ran me back to the parking lot, where she jumped into her car and sped off, **waving for me to follow**. (*Describe Courtney in a new way beginning with an* -ing *describer.*)

    —Rebecca Skloot, *The Immortal Life of Henrietta Lacks* (adapted)

2. <u>The room</u>, **shadowed well with awnings**, was dark and cool. (*Describe the room in a new way beginning with an* -ed *describer.*)

    —Christopher Paolini, *Eragon*

3. <u>The frozen earth</u> thawed, **leaving the short grass looking wet and weary**. (*Describe the earth in a new way beginning with an* -ing *describer.*)

    —Peter Abraham, *Tell Freedom*

4. **Standing in the clear sunshine**, <u>the prince</u> breathed in the sweet, fresh air. (*Describe the prince in a new way beginning with an* -ing *describer.*)

    —Sid Fleischman, *The Whipping Boy*

5. I shook my head, **disappointed**. (*Describe this person in a new way with just one word—an* -ed *describer.*)

    —Richard Wright, *Black Boy*

ACTIVITY 3: UNSCRAMBLING

Directions: Unscramble the sentence parts to imitate the model sentence. Start with the first sentence part listed. Write out the imitation sentence and <u>underline</u> the describer.

On the Mark: Put commas the same places as in the model sentence.

Model Sentence: Mr. Poe reached into his pocket for his handkerchief and, covering his mouth, coughed many, many times into it.

—Lemony Snicket, *The Bad Beginning*
(A Series of Unfortunate Events)

SENTENCE PARTS TO UNSCRAMBLE TO IMITATE THE MODEL SENTENCE

a. (*Start here.*) The cook

b. for her spatula

c. and

d. reached across the counter

e. flipped many, many pancakes with it

f. grabbing the utensil

IMITATION SENTENCE: The cook reached across the counter for her spatula and, grabbing the utensil, flipped many, many pancakes with it.

1. *Model Sentence:* Melodies, mixed with the soft smells of bedtime, slept with me.

—Sharon Draper, *Out of My Mind* (adapted)

a. (*Start here.*) Memories

b. washed over me

c. perfumed with the lovely fragrance of flowers

2. ***Model Sentence:*** Bea bustled about, managing to keep up with both the conversation and the cooking.

> —Eugenia Colier, "Sweet Potato Pie"

a. (*Start here.*) The helicopter arrived finally

b. within all the wreckage and crowds

c. trying to set down

3. ***Model Sentence:*** Alone with her grief, grappling with the horrible loss of her stillborn child, Leslie, the mother, in her own way was a lost child.

> —Damon Tweedy, *Black Man in a White Coat* (adapted)

a. (*Start here.*) Fearful of his enemies

b. Cranston, the guard, in his fear

c. struggling with the sickening realization of his obvious cowardice

d. was a poor protector

4. ***Model Sentence:*** In Texas, officers ran through the barracks at 4 a.m., screaming that Japanese planes were coming and ordering the cadets to **sprint** [*run*] outside and throw themselves on the ground.

> —Laura Hillenbrand, *Unbroken*

a. (*Start here.*) In New York

b. realizing that American lives were ending

c. bystanders looked at the World Trade Center at 10 A.M.

d. and wanting all witnesses to warn others and prevent casualties in the area

5. *Model Sentence:* Some older guys stood with their caps on backward, leaning against the fence, swirling basketballs on the tips of their fingers, waiting for all these crazy people to clear out so they could play. (*Contains three describers.*)

    —Toni Cade Bambara, "Raymond's Run"

    a. (*Start here.*) Some little fish sat with their camouflage on display

    b. hiding in the shadows

    c. hoping for all the bigger fish to move away so they could escape

    d. watching aggressive fish from the safety of their hiding places

ACTIVITY 4: COMBINING

Directions: Combine the bold parts into just one sentence that imitates the model. Write the imitation sentence and underline any describer tools. You'll learn that several weak sentences can be combined into just one strong sentence.

On the Mark: Put commas the same places as in the model sentence.

EXAMPLE

Model Sentence: He was running all-out now, dodging tree trunks and low-hanging branches as they loomed up suddenly in front of him. (*The describer tool is underlined.*)

    —Robert Ludlum, *The Moscow Vector* (adapted)

a. This is about **the plane**.

b. It **was falling down**.

c. Its fall was **suddenly**.

d. During its fall, it was **losing safe altitude**.

e. And it was **losing pressurized oxygen**.

f. This happened **as it bore down quickly toward tops of trees**.

Resulting Sentence: The plane was falling down suddenly, losing safe altitude and pressurized oxygen as it bore down quickly toward tops of trees. (*The describer tool is underlined.*)

----

1. *Model Sentence:* The ship's men were cold and hungry, soaked to the bone.

 —Hampton Sides, *In the Kingdom of Ice*

 a. The fuss was about **the dog's fur**.

 b. The fur **was matted and filthy**.

 c. It was **covered with** something.

 d. It was covered with **pond scum**.

2. *Model Sentence:* We began to save toward the trip north, plotting our time to set **tentative** [*possible*] dates for departure.

 —Richard Wright, *Black Boy*

 a. They hoped to do something.

 b. They wanted **to travel**.

 c. The travel would be **around the American South**.

 d. They planned on **visiting famous places**.

 e. Those visits were **to sample local food for meals**.

3. *Model Sentence:* Sitting patiently by a small fire, he snatched moths out of the air with his tongue when they flew too close to his face.

—Keith Donohue, *The Stolen Child*

a. He was **waiting hopefully on the landing dock**.

b. While he was waiting, **Carlos searched arrivers**.

c. The arrivers were **from the Ellis Island ship**.

d. He searched **for his family**.

e. He kept searching **as immigrants passed by his focused gaze**.

4. *Model Sentence:* Rivera was standing in the middle of the boxing ring with his feet flat on the lumpy canvas, planted like a tree.

—Robert Lipsyte, *The Contender*

a. **Storms were coming**.

b. They were coming **in the days of the hot summer**.

c. They came **with their rain heavy**.

d. The rain was **on the thirsty ground**.

e. It was **welcomed like a friend**.

5. *Model Sentence:* The pain hit me suddenly, doubling me over, racking my body with sobs. (*Contains two describers.*)

—Suzanne Collins, *The Hunger Games*

a. **The explosion shocked him**.

b. It shocked him **violently**.

c. It was **shaking him badly**.

d. It was **hurling his body**.

e. His body was hurled **through air**.

ACTIVITY 5: IMITATING

Directions: The model sentence and sample imitation contain describers and are built alike. Write an imitation sentence about something you know, something you've experienced, or something you've seen in the media. Read the model sentence, then its imitation, then your imitation. If all three are built pretty much alike, congratulations!

> **Tip:** Take it easy. Imitate one sentence part at a time because the best way to eat an elephant is one bite at a time. Here are the sentence parts of the model and its imitation.

Model Sentence Parts	Imitation Sentence Parts
1. a. The man toppled to one side,	**a.** The gymnast landed on one foot,
b. crumpling against the railing	**b.** balancing on the beam,
c. dead. —Robert Ludlum, *The Prometheus Deception*	**c.** triumphant.
2. a. While we held our breath,	**a.** As we watched the fish,
b. we pulled the sheets back	**b.** we observed the sharks circling
c. from the feet of the corpse,	**c.** around the back of the tank,
d. exposing the lower half of the torso. —Michael Crichton, *Travels*	**d.** threatening the smallest fish in the water.

3. a. Finally, **b.** the ship emerged entirely, **c.** bobbing on the **turbulent** (*rough*) water, **d.** and began to glide toward the bank. 　　—J. K. Rowling, *Harry Potter and the Goblet of Fire*	**a.** Suddenly, **b.** the whale submerged completely, **c.** disappearing into the ocean depth, **d.** and tried to escape from its hunters.
4. a. Through a thick window, **b.** they saw hundreds of fish **c.** all headed the same way, **d.** working their bodies hard **e.** but barely moving forward. 　　—Barbara Kingsolver, *Pigs in Heaven*	**a.** In the neighborhood gym, **b.** we witnessed lots of boxers **c.** all training for the big fight, **d.** practicing their skills daily **e.** and gradually getting better.
5. a. Mack and the boys, **b.** combed and cleaned, **c.** picked up their jugs, **d.** and marched down the chicken walk, **e.** over the railroad track, and through the lot across the street. 　　—John Steinbeck, *Cannery Row*	**a.** Athletes and their coaches, **b.** disciplined and trained, **c.** walked around the Olympic arena, **d.** and paraded before the cheering crowd, **e.** into the waiting cameras and among the teams from other nations.

ACTIVITY 6: EXPANDING

Directions: The describer has been removed from the author's sentence. At the caret (^), create a describer **several words long** that blends with the rest of the sentence.

EXAMPLE

Describer Removed

The medicine made her wander the house in the middle of the night like a zombie, ^ . (*In several words, describe how she was acting strangely, beginning with an* -ing *describer.*)

Your Describer

The medicine made her wander the house in the middle of the night like a zombie, **mumbling crazy comments about the roof caving in any minute.** (*Many others are possible to describe her.*)

Author's Describer

The medicine made her wander the house in the middle of the night like a zombie, **trying to cook breakfast by chopping cereal with a butcher knife.**
    —Rebecca Skloot, *The Immortal Life of Henrietta Lacks* (adapted)

---

1. The landlord, ^ , labored up the stairs. (*In several words, describe the landlord, beginning with an* -ing *describer.*)
        —Bernard Malamud, The Fixer

2. Dad steered the car through the dark, ^ . (*In several words, describe Dad, beginning with an* -ing *describer.*)
        —Jeanette Walls, *The Glass Castle*

3. Awake in his bed, ^ , Wesley began to shiver. (*In several words, describe Wesley, beginning with an -ing describer.*)

　　　　　　　　　　　　　　　—Stephen King, *Ur*

4. A man in a brown suit came toward her, ^ . (*In several words, describe the man, beginning with an -ing describer.*)

　　　　　　　　　　　　　　—Toni Morrison, *Song of Solomon*

5. Her brown face, ^ , was stained with tears. (*In several words, describe her unhappy face, beginning with an -ing describer.*)

　　　　　　　　　　　—Stephen Crane, *The Red Badge of Courage*

ACTIVITY 7: MULTIPLYING

Directions: The original sentence contained two or more describers. At the carets (^), create describers **several words long** that blend with the rest of the sentence. Describers begin with an *-ing* or *-ed* word.

EXAMPLE

Describers Removed
Tim hurried down the tree, ^ , ^ .

Your Describers
Tim hurried down the tree, **grabbing branches to hold, landing hard suddenly on the ground**. (*Many other describers are possible.*)

Author's Describers
Tim hurried down the tree, **slipping over the wet branches, feeling sticky sap on his hands**.

　　　　　　　　　　　　—Michael Crichton, *Jurassic Park*

1. Children love to play in piles of leaves, ^ , ^ .

    —Diane Ackerman, *A Natural History of the Senses*

2. ^ , ^ , Harry forced the goblet back toward Dumbledore's mouth and tipped it for Dumbledore to drink the remainder of the horrible poison inside.

    —J. K. Rowling, *Harry Potter and the Half-Blood Prince*

3. Outside, the snow, ^ , ^ , kept falling.

    —Kim Edwards, *The Memory Keeper's Daughter*

4. Dr. Garner did a quick medical exam, ^ , ^ , and ^ .

    —Damon Tweedy, *Black Man in a White Coat*

5. ^ , ^ , ^ , ^ , Calvin **strode** [*walked proudly*].

    —Rosa Guy, *The Friends* (adapted)

QUIZ: DESCRIBERS

Directions: Jot down whether the statement is true or false.

1. Describers are complete sentences.

2. All describers begin with a word ending in *-ing*.

3. This sentence contains three describers for the girls.

   The girls stood aside, talking among themselves, looking over their shoulders at the boys.
   —Shirley Jackson, "The Lottery"

4. This sentence has two describers, one beginning with an *-ing* word, the other with an *-ed* word.

   Blinded by the blaze of the spells that had blasted from every direction, deafened by a series of bangs, Harry blinked and looked down at the floor.
   —J. K. Rowling, *Harry Potter and the Goblet of Fire*

5. The best place for the describer is at the end of this sentence because there it describes the undertaker rather than the woman.

   Holding the mourners' hands, touching their arms, murmuring to them, she saw the undertaker standing near the hearse.

   She, **holding the mourners' hands, touching their arms, murmuring to them**, saw the undertaker standing near the hearse.

   She saw the undertaker standing near the hearse, **holding the mourners' hands, touching their arms, murmuring to them**.
   —Marilynne Robinson, *Lila*

MY WRITING: DESCRIBER TOOLS

Now it's your turn to use the describer tool to build your own terrific sentences. You've learned that this tool is great for describing people, places, or things.

Directions: Write six sentences about either famous people or famous places, or a mixture of both. The only must-have is a detailed describer in each sentence. Remember to begin your describers with a word ending in *-ing* or *-ed*.

Here are examples, with some describers at the beginning of the sentence, some in the middle, some at the end. Place your describers in any of those places.

Beginning Describer	Subject	Predicate
Famous Person **Elected for two consecutive terms as the American president,**	Barack Obama	was awarded the Nobel Peace Prize in 2009 for his efforts to improve international relations.
Famous Place **Entertaining an international group of tourists from every country in the world,**	Disney World in Florida	contains twenty-seven themed resort hotels, four theme parks, two water parks, several golf courses, and a camping resort.

Subject	Middle Describer	Predicate
Famous Person Muhammad Ali,	**making memorable comments such as "float like a butterfly, sting like a bee,"**	appeared on the cover of *Sports Illustrated* thirty-seven times.
Famous Place One World Trade Center,	**standing now as the crown jewel of the New York City skyline,**	was erected on the site of the twin towers that were destroyed in terrorist attacks on September 11, 2001.

Subject	Predicate	End Describer
Famous Person The amazingly popular Harry Potter novels	earned multimillions of dollars for first-time novelist J. K. Rowling,	**published after a series of rejections by many publishers.**
Famous Place Times Square in New York City	attracts millions of tourists annually,	**entertaining them with Broadway shows, tourist shops, spectacular hotels, and fine restaurants.**

ELABORATOR TOOL

Elaborators (absolutes) are sentence parts that give additional details about people, places, or things. Elaborators usually begin with one of these words: *my*, *his*, *her*, *its*, *our*, *their*. Elaborators can appear in a sentence at the beginning, middle, or end.

Read the following sentence pairs. The elaborators are **bolded**, and what they tell more about is <u>underlined</u>. These sentences show how elaborators build better sentences.

1a. The student walked to the front of the room where she faced the class.

1b. Her back to the teacher, <u>the student</u> walked to the front of the room where she faced the class. (*Elaborator is at the beginning.*)
  —Rosa Guy, *The Friends*

2a. A thick scarf was crossed over his chest.

2b. <u>A thick scarf</u>, **its ends tucked into his coat**, was crossed over his chest. (*Elaborator is in the middle.*)
  —Leslie Morris, "Three Shots for Charlie Beston"

3a. A blond little boy looked very small sitting there alone in the big old-fashioned kitchen.

3b. <u>A blond little boy</u> looked very small sitting there alone in the big old-fashioned kitchen, **his feet swinging a good six inches above the floor**. (*Elaborator is at the end.*)
  —Madeleine L'Engle, *A Wrinkle in Time*

Important: Elaborators are sentence parts that are *almost* complete sentences. If elaborators contained *was* or *were*, they would be sentences, not elaborators. Test each underlined elaborator by adding *was* or *were* to make the elaborator into a complete sentence.

EXAMPLES

1. Jones was thin and graying, his deep voice softened by a faint Southern accent.

      —Rebecca Skloot, *The Immortal Life of Henrietta Lacks*

   <u>Test</u>: His deep voice WAS softened by a faint Southern accent.

2. She sat down, <u>her fingers tightening on the container.</u>

      —Robert Lipsyte, *The Contender*

   <u>Test</u>: Her fingers WERE tightening on the container.

3. <u>His fingers hurting</u>, Taran hurried from the cottage and found Coll near the vegetable garden.

      —Lloyd Alexander, *The Book of Three (adapted)*

   <u>Test</u>: His fingers WERE hurting.

4. Grant saw the head of an animal, motionless, <u>its two large dark eyes watching him coldly.</u>

      —Michael Crichton, *Jurassic Park* (adapted)

   <u>Test</u>: Its two large dark eyes WERE watching him coldly.

5. They walked in silence, <u>their eyes on the ground.</u>

      —J. K. Rowling, *Harry Potter and the Sorcerer's Stone*

   <u>Test</u>: Their eyes WERE on the ground.

ACTIVITY 1: MATCHING

Directions: Insert the elaborator into the sentence at the caret (^). To practice using the elaborator tool, copy and punctuate the sentence.

Sentence	Elaborator
1. Cliff and Fred stood wet in the graveyard behind the house, ^ . —Rebecca Skloot, *The Immortal Life of Henrietta Lacks*	**a.** her hands on her hips
2. I spent the day at the hospital, ^ . —Jacqueline Woodson, *Another Brooklyn*	**b.** his back propped against a pile of pillows
3. ^, the little boy made the paper boat sitting up in bed. —Stephen King, *It*	**c.** their **overalls** [*pants*] **drenched** [*soaked*] and heavy with rain
4. The tyrannosaur stood near the front of the Land Cruiser, ^ . —Michael Crichton, *Jurassic Park* (adapted)	**d.** my father moaning for pain medication
5. Mrs. Weasley, ^, came to a **halt** [*stop*] in front of them and stared from one guilty face to the next. —J. K. Rowling, *Harry Potter and the Chamber of Secrets*	**e.** its arms making clawing movements in the air

ACTIVITY 2: EXCHANGING

Directions: Replace the elaborator with one of yours that fits the rest of the sentence. Make your elaborator about the same length as the author's elaborator. Begin your elaborator with one of these words: *my, his, her, its, our, their.* The elaborators are **bolded**, and what they tell more about is underlined.

EXAMPLE

Author's Elaborator

On the road was <u>the man from the night before</u>, **his black hat on his head**.

> —Natalie Babbitt, *Tuck Everlasting*

Your Elaborator

On the road was <u>the man from the night before</u>, **his red car shining brightly**. (*Many other elaborators are possible.*)

---

1. <u>Mother</u> looked neither right nor left, **her eyes staring straight ahead**. (*Elaborate on Mother with new information beginning with the word* her.)

   > —Robert Lipsyte, *The Contender* (adapted)

2. <u>His classmate and Damon</u> were sitting in the **faculty** [*teacher*] lounge, **their eyes on the twenty-five-inch TV**. (*Elaborate on the classmate and Damon with new information beginning with the word* their.)

   > —Damon Tweedy, *Black Man in a White Coat*

3. <u>A man</u>, **his clothes fuming where the blast had blown out the fire**, rose from the curb. (*Elaborate on the burned man with new information beginning with the word* his.)

   > —Fritz Leiber, "A Bad Day for Sales"

4. I squeeze through sweaty bodies and follow <u>Kenya</u>, **her curls bouncing past her shoulders**. (*Elaborate on Kenya with new information beginning with the word* her.)

   > —Angie Thomas, *The Hate U Give*

5. The snake **slithered** [*crawled*] straight toward Justin and raised itself **poised** [*ready*] to strike, **its fangs exposed**. (*Elaborate on the snake with new information beginning with the word* its.)
    —J. K. Rowling, *Harry Potter and the Chamber of Secrets* (adapted)

ACTIVITY 3: UNSCRAMBLING

Directions: Unscramble the sentence parts to imitate the model sentence. Start with the first sentence part listed. Write out the imitation sentence and underline the elaborator.

On the Mark: Put commas the same places as in the model sentence.

EXAMPLE

Model Sentence: Unoka played his flute with the village musicians, his face beaming with blessedness and peace.
    —Chinua Achebe, *Things Fall Apart*

SENTENCE PARTS TO UNSCRAMBLE TO IMITATE THE MODEL SENTENCE

    a. (*Start here.*) The squid moved its body

    b. through the murky water

    c. curiosity and hunger

    d. its tentacles exploring from

Imitation Sentence The squid moved its body through the murky water, its tentacles exploring from curiosity and hunger.

1. *Model Sentence:* The beautiful animal stood still, its head toward the man sitting on an upturned bucket outside the cage.

   —J. K. Rowling, *Harry Potter and the Chamber of Secrets*

   a. (*Start here.*) A refugee yelled there

   b. waiting on the New York dock

   c. near the ship

   d. his arms waving toward his brother

2. *Model Sentence:* His father found him lying drunk in their yard, his shirt soaked with blood.

   —Rebecca Skloot, *The Immortal Life of Henrietta Lack*

   a. (*Start here.*) Her father

   b. her voice filled with joy

   c. saw his daughter

   d. playing happily in the yard

3. *Model Sentence:* Several spiders were thrown onto their backs, their endless legs waving in the air.

   —J. K. Rowling, *Harry Potter and the Chamber of Secrets*

   a. (*Start here.*) Five inmates

   b. into their cells

   c. their protesting screams echoing through the prison

   d. were shoved

4. In the morning he went in, bought a bag of some gumdrops, and went up the street, his mouth full of candy.

   —Hal Borland, *When the Legends Die (adapted)*

   a. (*Start here.*) Near the driveway the dog turned around

   b. its tail wagging with excitement

   c. and ran toward the man

   d. noticed its owner near the truck

5. *Model Sentence:* Whenever he had a moment to sit, he could usually be found smoking a fancy pipe, his head buried in a book.

   —Hampton Sides, *In the Kingdom of Ice*

   a. (*Start here.*) After she spent much time to research

   b. her mind engaged in the plot

   c. Agatha Christie could often be seen

   d. writing a detective story

ACTIVITY 4: COMBINING

Directions: Combine the **bold** parts into just one sentence that imitates the model. Write the imitation sentence and underline any elaborator tools. You'll learn that several weak sentences can be combined into just one strong sentence.

On the Mark: Put commas the same places as in the model sentence.

EXAMPLE

Model Sentence: Then came a blast of wind so strong it tore the metal roof off the barn, <u>its long metal slopes flapping like the wings of a giant bird</u>. (*The elaborator tool is underlined.*)
 —Rebecca Skloot, *The Immortal Life of Henrietta Lack (adapted)*

a. Soon came a sound of thunder.

b. It was **so loud**.

c. It scattered the picnic gathering.

d. That gathering went **into the house**.

e. Its explosive terrifying clap was **sounding like the roar**.

f. The roar was **of a prehistoric animal**.

Resulting Sentence: Soon came a sound of thunder so loud it scattered the picnic gathering into the house, <u>its explosive terrifying clap sounding like the roar of a prehistoric animal</u>. (*The elaborator tool is underlined.*)

---

1. *Model Sentence:* Eugie came clomping down the stairs and into the kitchen, <u>his head drooping with sleepiness</u>.
 —Gina Berriault, "The Stone Boy"

   a. Pam started stirring around the stew.

   b. And she stirred **within the sauce**.

   c. When she did this, **her recipe** was **smelling of cloves**.

2. *Model Sentence:* Pushing himself up, his pain throbbing in his legs, he looked around.

    —Robb White, *Deathwatch*

    a. She was **covering herself over**.

    b. **Her chills** were **pulsing**.

    c. They were pulsing **through her body**.

    d. **Rosa sat down**.

3. *Model Sentence:* Six boys came over the hill with heads down, their breaths whistling.

    —John Steinbeck, *The Red Pony* (adapted)

    a. **Thousands of termites crawled**.

    b. They crawled **over the hut**.

    c. They crawled **with hunger strong**.

    d. **Their colonies** were **swarming**.

4. *Model Sentence:* Henrietta's corpse lay in the hallway of the house, its doors propped open at each end to let in the cool wet breeze that would keep her body fresh.

    —Rebecca Skloot, *The Immortal Life of Henrietta Lack*

    a. **Melissa's baby was in the crib in the nursery**.

    b. **Its mobiles** were **placed overhead**.

    c. They were **at various heights**.

    d. The mobiles were there **to make for some attractions**.

    e. Those attractions were the kind **that would keep the baby amused**.

5. *Model Sentence:* <u>His feet sinking in the soft carpet with his hand in one pocket</u>, he felt as if he could squeal or laugh.

> —Theodore Dreiser, *An American Tragedy* (adapted)

   a. **Its movement** was **hidden**.

   b. The movement was hidden **by the jungle plants**.

   c. It moved **with its head nearing the soldier**.

   d. **The cobra looked as if** it would do something.

   e. It looked as if **it would rear and strike**.

ACTIVITY 5: IMITATING

Directions: The model sentence and sample imitation contain elaborators and are built alike. Write an imitation sentence about something you know, something you've experienced, or something you've seen on media. Read the model sentence, then its imitation, then your imitation. If all three are built pretty much alike, congratulations!

> **Tip:** Take it easy. Imitate one sentence part at a time. Here are the sentence parts of the model and its imitation.

Model Sentence Parts	Imitation Sentence Parts
1. a. The undertaker inched through the field	**a.** The snake crawled through the crack
b. between the road and the house,	**b.** near the cellar and the shed,
c. his tires sinking into puddles of mud.	**c.** its movement speeded by barks from our dog.
—Rebecca Skloot, *The Immortal Life of Henrietta Lacks*	

2. a. Scores of workers **b.** had been hurt or killed **c.** in building the world's fair, **d.** their families **consigned** [*destined*] to poverty. —Eric Larson, *The Devil in the White City*	**a.** Lots of buildings **b.** had been damaged or destroyed **c.** in experiencing the strong storm, **d.** their architecture reduced to ruins.
3. a. He handed me a bound black notebook, **b.** its pages lined **c.** to ensure the **proper** [*correct*] placement **d.** of words and sentences. —Keith Donohue, *The Stolen Child* (adapted)	**a.** The class gave him a large gold medal, **b.** its surface inscribed **c.** to honor his outstanding achievement **d.** in math and science.
4. a. Jonas's ankle was twisted, **b.** and his knees were scraped and raw, **c.** his blood **seeping** [*leaking*] **d.** through his torn trousers. —Lois Lowry, *The Giver*	**a.** Her garden was full, **b.** and its flowers were blooming and abundant, **c.** their fragrance **drifting** **d.** through the lovely garden.
5. a. On election night, **b.** before Blaine kissed her, **c.** his face wet with tears, **d.** he held her tightly **e.** as though Obama's victory was also their personal victory. —Chimamanda Ngozi Adichie, *Americanah*	**a.** On Halloween night, **b.** after Mom costumed Gabriela, **c.** her face hidden by feathers, **d.** the child hugged her happily **e.** as if her costume was definitely the absolute best.

ACTIVITY 6: EXPANDING

Directions: The elaborator has been removed from the author's sentence. At the caret (^), create an elaborator **several words long** that blends with the rest of the sentence.

EXAMPLE

Elaborator Removed

Far down the line a few children stood and stared at the newly arrived truck, **their ^** .

Your Elaborator

Far down the line a few children stood and stared at the newly arrived truck, **their bodies still wet from the pool**. (*Many other elaborators are possible.*)

Author's Elaborator

Far down the line a few children stood and stared at the newly arrived truck, **their hair gray with dust**.

        —John Steinbeck, *The Grapes of Wrath*

1. Calvin led the way to the wall and then sat there, **his ^** . (*In several words, tell more about Calvin.*)

        —Madeleine L'Engle, *A Wrinkle in Time*

2. As the ship came closer, **its ^** , he kept watching it. (*In several words, tell more about the ship.*)

        —Scott O'Dell, *Island of the Blue Dolphins*

3. Across a narrow little office sat a young man in work clothes, **his** ^ . (*In several words, tell more about the young man.*)

      —Jack Finney, "Of Missing Persons"

4. Big, rough teenagers jostled through the crowd, **their** ^ . (*In several words, tell more the teenagers.*)

      —Robert Lipsyte, *The Contender*

5. She burst into great sobs, **her** ^ . (*In several words, tell more about her sobs.*)

      —Michael Crichton, *Travels* (adapted)

ACTIVITY 7: MULTIPLYING

Directions: The original sentence contained two or more elaborators. At the carets (^), create elaborators **several words long** that blend with the rest of the sentence. Most elaborators begin with one of these words: *my, his, her, its, our, their*.

EXAMPLE

Elaborators Removed
The fallen rider twitched once and lay motionless, **his** ^ , **his** ^ .
      —Khaled Hosseini, *The Kite Runner* (adapted)

Your Elaborator
The fallen rider twitched once and lay motionless, **his eyes closed, his breathing stopped**. (*Many other elaborators are possible.*)

Author's Elaborator

The fallen rider twitched once and lay motionless, **his legs bent at unnatural angles, his blood soaking through the sand.**

—Khaled Hosseini, *The Kite Runner* (adapted)

---

1. Chris was beside me, **his ^** , **his ^** .

   —Stephen King, "The Body"

2. **Her ^** , **her ^** , she went outside and sat on the step.

   —Hal Borland, *When the Legends Die*

3. **His ^** and **his ^** , he lifted the truck in one powerful motion until the front was several inches off the ground.

   —Mildred D. Taylor, *Roll of Thunder, Hear My Cry* (adapted)

4. **His ^** , Harry saw that what had hold of him was marching on six immensely long, hairy legs, **its ^** .

   —J. K. Rowling, *Harry Potter and the Chamber of Secrets*

5. The wolf was almost as big as a calf, **its ^** , **its ^** , **its ^** .

   —Stephen King, *Just After Sunset*

QUIZ: ELABORATORS

Directions: Jot down whether the statement is true or false.

1. Elaborators are complete sentences.

2. Most elaborators begin with one of these words—*my, his, her, its, our, their*.

3. The imitation sentence does not match the arrangement of the elaborators in the model sentence.

    Model Sentence: Mama sat back, her hand still in Papa's, her eyes **wary** [*cautious*].

    —Mildred D. Taylor, *Roll of Thunder, Hear My Cry*

    Imitation Sentence: His heart pounding, Dad looked around, his son still in danger.

4. This sentence has more than two elaborators.

    Neville, his face tear-streaked, clutching his wrist, hobbled off with Madame Hooch, who had her arm around him.

    —J. K. Rowling, *Harry Potter and the Sorcerer's Stone*

5. Elaborators never occur at the end of a sentence.

MY WRITING: ELABORATOR TOOLS

Now it's your turn to use the elaborator tool to build your own terrific sentences. You've learned that this tool is great for telling more about people, places, or things.

Directions: Write six sentences about either famous people or famous places, or a mixture of both. The only must-have is a detailed elaborator in each sentence. Remember to begin your elaborators with one of these words: *my, his, her, its, our, their*.

Here are examples, with some elaborators at the *beginning* of the sentence, some in the *middle*, some at the *end*. Place your elaborators in any of those places.

Beginning Elaborator	Subject	Predicate
Famous Person **His Harvard education a good preparation,**	Barack Obama	was awarded the Nobel Peace Prize in 2009 for his efforts to improve international relations.
Famous Place **Its underground tunnels for use by employees only,**	Disney World in Florida	contains twenty-seven themed resort hotels, four theme parks, two water parks, several golf courses, and a camping resort.

Subject	Middle Elaborator	Predicate
Famous Person Muhammad Ali,	**his style as much dancing as boxing,**	appeared on the cover of *Sports Illustrated* thirty-seven times.
Famous Place One World Trade Center,	**its presence an important symbol on the New York City skyline,**	was erected on the site of the twin towers destroyed in terrorist attacks on September 11, 2001.

Subject	Predicate	End Elaborator
Famous Person The amazingly popular Harry Potter novels	earned multimillions of dollars for first-time novelist J. K. Rowling,	**her life forever changed by this success.**
Famous Place Times Square in New York City	attracts millions of tourists annually,	**its giant neon signs flashing news, entertainment, and advertising.**

REVIEW: THE SENTENCE-COMPOSING POWER TOOLS

Congratulations on learning, practicing, and using these powerful sentence-composing tools: *extender*, *identifier*, *describer*, *elaborator*. Like all good writers, you'll want to take them out of your sentence-composing toolbox to build strong sentences for just about everything you write.

Good writers use those same tools in books and magazines, blogs and websites, novels and essays, articles and speeches and letters.

Here is one example among thousands and thousands of good writers. One popular author is John Steinbeck. The following review activities show how he uses those tools in one of his novels: *Of Mice and Men*. It is a story of two friends, George and Lennie, who travel and work together, but encounter difficulties because Lennie, with the body of a giant but the mind of a child, innocently gets them into trouble.

Directions: Identify the underlined tools. If you need to review them, study the following pages.

Tool	Review These Pages
extender	pages 44–59
identifier	pages 60–75
describer	pages 76–93
elaborator	pages 94–110

REVIEW 1: NAMING THE TOOLS

Directions: Write the name of the underlined tool.

1. George, sitting on the bunk beside Lennie, frowned as he thought.

2. As the blaze dropped from the fire, the **sphere** [*circle*] of light grew smaller.

3. A water snake slipped along on the pool, its head held up like a little periscope.

4. Raising his eyes, Crooks stiffened, and a **scowl** [*frown*] came on his face.

5. George stood still, watching the angry little man.

6. At that moment a young man came into the bunk house, a thin young man with a brown face, brown eyes and a head of tightly curled hair.

7. Near one wall there was a black cast iron stove, its stovepipe going straight up through the ceiling.

8. Lennie got quiet, grumbling to himself about threatening the future cats which might dare to disturb the future rabbits.

9. Behind George walked his opposite, a huge man with wide sloping shoulders and shapeless face and large, pale eyes.

10. Curley's wife stood still in the doorway, smiling a little at them while rubbing the nails of one hand with the thumb and forefinger of the other.

REVIEW 2: IMITATING JOHN STEINBECK'S SENTENCES

Directions: For each model sentence, write the letter of its imitation. Then write your own imitation of the same model. The tools are underlined and named.

MODEL SENTENCES

1. Noiselessly, Lennie appeared in the open doorway and stood there looking in, his big shoulders nearly filling the opening. (*elaborator*)

2. He unrolled his **bindle** [*sack*] and put things on the shelf, the razor and a bar of soap, the comb and bottle of pills, the liniment and leather wristband. (*identifiers*)

3. The dog struggled lamely to the side of the room and lay down, <u>grunting softly to himself and licking his grizzled, moth-eaten coat.</u> (*describers*)

4. Old Candy, <u>the handyman</u> (*identifier*), came in and went to his bunk, and behind him struggled his old dog.

5. Lennie drank with long gulps from the surface of the green pool, <u>snorting into the water like a horse.</u> (*describer*)

IMITATION SENTENCES

A. Little Mattie, the youngest, toddled over and sat on the sofa, and beside her was her older sister.

B. Susan ate with small bites from the plate on the kitchen table, picking over the food like a bird.

C. She got out her bag and gathered items for the weekend, the bathing suit and a bottle of suntan lotion, the shorts, a case with makeup, a shirt, and the team sweatshirt.

D. Gleefully, Maya ran through the sprinkler, and ran back lingering inside, her tiny feet always running in place.

E. The diver walked carefully to the end of the board and balanced there, talking inwardly to himself and rehearsing his difficult championship dive.

COMBO TOOL

Mash-up, medley, assortment, combination, array, mixture, miscellany, potpourri, variety, smorgasbord—all of them are about the lack of sameness and monotony. All are about variety.

The saying "Variety is the spice of life" applies also to sentences. The spice aisle in a food store has hundreds of different flavors—salt, pepper, turmeric, and cardamom—because in their food people like flavor.

In their sentences, too, people like flavor. A powerful tool that adds spice and flavor to sentences is the combo tool. It includes at least two tools you already know—*the extender, the identifier, the describer, the elaborator*—within the same sentence.

Read the following sentence pairs. The first sentence has no combo. The second has a combo. The combo provides more information.

1a. Paintings of his ancestors lined the hallway.

1b. Paintings of his ancestors, **the family who had ruled Austria for six hundred years**, lined the hallway, **their faces staring down with unreadable expressions**. (*Combo contains an identifier and an elaborator.*)
           —Scott Westerfield, *Leviathan*

2a. High above him was a solid wall of spiders.

2b. High above him was a solid wall of spiders, **clicking, their many eyes gleaming in their ugly black heads**. (*Combo contains a describer and an elaborator.*)
      —J. K. Rowling, *Harry Potter and the Chamber of Secrets* (adapted)

3a. Charles Wallace looked very small sitting there alone in the big old-fashioned kitchen.

3b. When he sat there alone in the big old-fashioned kitchen, Charles Wallace looked very small, **a blond little boy in faded blue denims, his feet swinging a good six inches above the floor**. (*Combo contains an extender, an identifier, and an elaborator.*)

—Madeleine L'Engle, *A Wrinkle in Time*

4a. Georgie walked down the four steps to the cellar shelf, sure that at any moment the cellar door would swing shut on its own, and then he would hear IT.

4b. Georgie walked down the four steps to the cellar shelf, **his heart a beating hammer in his throat, his hair on the nape of his neck standing at attention, his eyes hot, his hands cold**, sure that at any moment the cellar door would swing shut on its own, **closing off the white light falling through the kitchen windows**, and then he would hear IT, **the monster growling deeply in those seconds before it pounced on him and unzipped his guts**. (*Combo contains four elaborators, one describer, one identifier.*)

—Stephen King, *It*

ACTIVITY 1: IDENTIFYING COMBOS

Each sentence has a combo of three different tools. Copy the sentence, and underline and name each tool in parentheses.

EXAMPLE

A beautiful college student with short blond hair (*identifier*), she sat in a rocking chair, her long legs curled under her (*elaborator*), looking very calm and composed (*describer*).

—Michael Crichton, *Travels*

Note: To review the tools, see these pages.

The Extender	pages 44–59
The Identifier	pages 60–75
The Describer	pages 76–93
The Elaborator	pages 94–110

---

1. A weakened man, he fell back, exhausted, his ankle pounding.

    —Ralph Ellison, "Flying Home"

2. He viewed photographs, a collection of pictures of soldiers, their arms on one another's shoulders, standing in uniforms against the background of the sea.

    —Roya Hakakian, *Journey from the Land of No* (adapted)

3. She had one good friend in town, a Puerto Rican woman named Lupe, her age around seventy, dressed always in too-tight clothes on her large body.

    —Oscar Hijuelos, *The Fourteen Sisters of Emilio Montez O'Brien*

4. While I was resting there, sucking the juice from the cactus, I saw the big gray dog, the leader of the wild pack, in the brush above me.

    —Scott O'Dell, *Island of Blue Dolphins*

5. As the wind kicked up around him, ripping the wrapping paper out of his hands, my brother, his hands gripping the edge of the picnic table, saw the paper sail upward with all the balloons from the party.

    —Ingrid Law, *Savvy*

ACTIVITY 2: ARRANGING COMBOS

Directions: The combo has been removed from each sentence. A list of tools is underneath each sentence. Copy the sentence, and then insert the tools into acceptable places. <u>Underline</u> and name each tool in parentheses: *extender*, *identifier*, *describer*, or *elaborator*.

On the Mark: Tools need commas that separate them from the rest of the sentence.

EXAMPLE

- In the far corner, the man was still asleep.
- snoring slightly on the intaking breath
- his head back against the wall

SAMPLE ARRANGEMENTS

a. In the far corner, <u>his head back against the wall</u> (*elaborator*), the man was still asleep, <u>snoring slightly on the intaking breath</u> (*describer*).

b. In the far corner, <u>snoring slightly on the intaking breath</u> (*describer*), <u>his head back against the wall</u> (*elaborator*), the man was still asleep.

c. In the far corner, <u>snoring slightly on the intaking breath</u> (*describer*), the man was still asleep, <u>his head back against the wall</u> (*elaborator*).

d. <u>His head back against the wall</u> (*elaborator*), in the far corner, the man, <u>snoring slightly on the intaking breath</u> (*describer*), was still asleep.

e. <u>Snoring slightly on the intaking breath</u> (*describer*), <u>his head back against the wall</u> (*elaborator*), in the far corner, the man was still asleep.

ORIGINAL SENTENCE

In the far corner, the man was still asleep, <u>snoring slightly on the intaking breath</u> (*describer*), <u>his head back against the wall</u> (*elaborator*).

> —Ernest Hemingway, "The Undefeated"

Note: The tools underneath the sentences are arranged randomly. There is more than one good arrangement for the combo tools. If the sentence makes sense, it is a good arrangement.

1. I rushed into Mama's room.

    > —Mildred D. Taylor, *Roll of Thunder, Hear My Cry*

    - my feet barely hitting the rug

    - jumping from the bed

2. Harry looked straight into the snake's face and saw that its eyes had been punctured by the **phoenix** [*magical bird*].

    > —J. K. Rowling, *Harry Potter and the Chamber of Secrets*

    - its blood streaming the floor

    - the great, **bulbous** [*round*] yellow eyes

3. Ray-Ray leaped into the air, but the ball was way over his head.

    > —Murray Heyert, "The New Kid"

    - a mom with a baby carriage

    - bouncing beyond him on the sidewalk near a woman

    - his arms up

4. Polly Chalmers was standing out on the sidewalk.
> —Stephen King, *Needful Things*

- looking at the awning with an expression that seemed puzzled
- the lady who ran the sewing shop
- her hands on her admirably slim hips

5. Phyllis was with her father.
> —Frank McCourt, *Teacher Man* (adapted)

- when her mother called her to come and see Neil Armstrong
- wanting though not to miss the historic moon landing
- worried about her father who was dying in the bedroom
- the first person to set foot on the moon

ACTIVITY 3: COMBINING

Directions: Make the **bold** parts a combo to insert at the carets (^) in the first sentence. Underline and name each tool in parentheses: *extender*, *identifier*, *describer*, or *elaborator*.

On the Mark: Tools need commas that separate them from the rest of the sentence.

EXAMPLE

Grandpa waved his hat, ^ , ^ . He was **trying to head the horse off**. His waving was with **his arms whirling like a windmill**.

Combined: Grandpa waved his hat, trying to head the horse off [*describer*], his arms whirling like a windmill [*elaborator*].
> —Marguerite Henry, *Misty of Chincoteague*

1. I started making an iceball, ^ , ^ . It was **a perfect one from perfectly white snow**. The iceball was **squeezed perfectly clear so no snow remained all the way through**.

   —Annie Dillard, *An American Childhood* (adapted)

2. After the tyrannosaur's head crashed against the hood of the Land Cruiser and shattered the windshield, Tim was knocked flat on the seat, ^ , ^ . Tim was **blinking in the darkness**. His face showed **his mouth warm with blood**.

   —Michael Crichton, *Jurassic Park*

3. ^ , the digger wasps give off a strong odor, ^ . This happens when the wasps are **excited by a nearby spider**. The odor is **a warning that they are ready to attack**.

   —Alexander Petrunkevitch, "The Spider and the Wasp"

4. Boo Boo Tannenbaum, ^ , came into the kitchen, ^ , ^ . Boo Boo was **the lady of the house**. She was **a small, almost hipless girl of twenty-five**. She was **dressed in knee-length jeans and a black turtleneck pullover**.

   —J. D. Salinger, "Down at the Dinghy"

5. Harry twisted his body around and saw a grindylow, ^, ^, ^, ^. A grindylow is **a small, horned water demon**. It was **poking out of the weed**. It had **its long fingers clutched tightly around Harry's leg**. It had **its pointed fangs bared**.

   —J. K. Rowling, *Harry Potter and the Goblet of Fire*

ACTIVITY 4: IMITATING

Directions: Each model sentence contains a combo. Find and copy its imitation built like the model. Then imitate the same model, built the same way as the model sentence and its imitation sentence. Write your imitation sentence about something you know, something you've experienced, or something you've seen in the media.

GROUP 1: MODEL SENTENCES

1. A short, round boy of seven, he took little interest in troublesome things, preferring to remain on good terms with everyone.
   —Mildred D. Taylor, *Roll of Thunder, Hear My Cry*

2. Married at an early age, an unspotted lamb, she had been accepted by a good family of strict Spaniards whose name was old and respected.
   —Judith Ortiz Cofer, *Silent Dancing* (adapted)

3. I kept my eyes on my hands on the desk, waiting for something to happen, an explosion, a battle cry, a noise, anything but the silence.
   —Rosa Guy, *The Friends*

4. There stood Dr. Zohreh Abedinzadeh, the chief of the nation's atomic experts, surrounded by men in white coats.
   —Roya Hakakian, *Journey from the Land of No*

5. The photographer, a novice with a local paper who had gotten a tip that a movie star's wife and child had perished in the fire, stepped back, stunned and ashamed.
   —Oscar Hijuelos, *The Fourteen Sisters of Emilio Montez O'Brien*

GROUP 1: IMITATIONS

A. Trophied as a champion swimmer, an unprecedented Olympian, Michael Phelps had been raised by a single mother with great care, whose support was solid and constant.

B. Then appeared Johnny Unitas, the star quarterback of the NFL's Baltimore Colts, lifted by teammates in thrilling victory.

C. The tornado devastated the mall on the outskirts of the town, hitting with destruction to buildings, a movie, a department store, a McDonald's, everything within its path.

D. A rotund, respected leader of Britain, Churchill liked his liquor in most settings, wanting to drink at various hours of the day.

E. Secretariat, a thoroughbred with an excellent pedigree who had earned a reputation that a housewife and trainer had developed with expert care, raced hard, energized and determined.

GROUP 2: MODEL SENTENCES

6. Ray-Ray leaped into the air, his arms flung up, but the ball was way over his head, bouncing beyond him on the sidewalk near a woman, a mom jouncing a baby carriage at the door of the apartment house opposite.

> —Murray Heyert, "The New Kid" (adapted)

7. My father was an intimidating giant of a man, a former college football player, standing six foot two and 245 pounds, with thick, meaty hands, his every finger broken and bent.

> —Perri Knize, *A Piano Odyssey*

8. I was suddenly silent, my breath snatched from me, replaced by a **melancholy** [*sadness*] my family couldn't understand.

> —Jacqueline Woodson, *Another Brooklyn* (adapted)

9. I didn't recognize her in the cover photograph, a **plump** [*large*] woman with big round glasses, sitting beside him in the football stadium, their knees covered by a single plaid blanket.

   —Tobias Wolff, *Old School* (adapted)

10. Suffering a crippling stroke at age thirty-nine, Jim was another casualty of inequality, a fresh example of the health burden of being black.

    —Damon Tweedy, *Black Man in a White Coat*

GROUP 2: IMITATIONS

F. Eating over a lifetime about fifty tons, people are an astonishment of biology, a huge indicator of the amazing accomplishments of human bodies.

G. I reminisced about him during the long summer, a cute lacrosse player with dazzling blue eyes, laughing with me in the crowded cafeteria, our laughter fueled by two contented happy hearts.

H. Janine was frequently excited, her dreams fueled by success, motivated by a power my coaches loved watching.

I. Carmela walked onto the stage, her voice warmed up, but the audience was distracted from her performance, staring around them at a man in the balcony, a heckler yelling a loud remark in the middle of her opening song onstage.

J. My sister was a little slip of a woman, a very talented college gymnast, wearing dark tights and ponytail, with admirable, stunning grace, her muscles toned and firm.

ACTIVITY 5: CREATING COMBOS

Create a combo of the tools in CAPITALS and insert them in places indicated.

EXAMPLE

> *Incomplete Sentence:* Harry watched, DESCRIBER, as a **portly** [*fat*] ghost approached the table, crouched low, and walked through it, ELABORATOR .

> *Sample Combo:* Harry watched, <u>fascinated by the sight</u>, as a portly ghost approached the table, crouched low, and walked through it, <u>its shape vanishing quickly</u>.

> *Original:* Harry watched, <u>amazed at the scene</u>, as a portly ghost approached the table, crouched low, and walked through it, <u>its mouth held wide so that it passed through one of the stinking salmon</u>.

> —J. K. Rowling, *Harry Potter and the Chamber of Secrets*

---

1. DESCRIBER, the wild dog stood facing me, ELABORATOR.
   —Scott O'Dell, *Island of Blue Dolphins* (adapted)

2. The medicine made her wander the house in the middle of the night like a zombie, DESCRIBER, ELABORATOR.
   —Rebecca Skloot, *The Immortal Life of Henrietta Lacks* (adapted)

3. IDENTIFIER, Ben had been my best friend since fifth grade, EXTENDER.
   —John Green, *Paper Towns*

4. The dead rider, DESCRIBER, lay motionless, ELABORATOR, ELABORATOR.

>—Khaled Hosseini, *The Kite Runner*

5. Carrie, IDENTIFIER, was a chunky girl with pimples on her neck and back and buttocks, DESCRIBER, ELABORATOR.

>—Stephen King, *Carrie* (adapted)

THE TOOLBOX

To get the job done right, use the right tools. You've learned five of the right tools to build stronger sentences: *the extender*, *the identifier*, *the describer*, *the elaborator*, *the combo*. Those power tools are in your toolbox. Now get ready to use them in this section by building strong sentences. When you finish, admire your work, done right with the right sentence-composing tools, and take a bow!

ACTIVITY 1: PLACING TOOLS

Following are sentences from earlier in this worktext. Under each sentence are tools from those sentences.

Part One Directions: Add *one* of the tools in a good place in the sentence. Copy the sentence and underline the tool you inserted.

On the Mark: Use a comma to separate the tool from the rest of the sentence.

1. Barack Obama was awarded the Nobel Peace Prize in 2009 for his efforts to improve international relations.

   • EXTENDER: when he was a newly elected president in 2009

   • IDENTIFIER: the first African-American president of the United States of America

   • DESCRIBER: elected for two consecutive terms as the American president

   • ELABORATOR: his Harvard education a good preparation

2. Disney World in Florida contains twenty-seven themed resort hotels, four theme parks, two water parks, several golf courses, and a camping resort.

   - EXTENDER: since it was designed to surpass Disneyland in California

   - IDENTIFIER: the most visited vacation resort in the world with an estimated fifty-two million visitors annually

   - DESCRIBER: entertaining an international group of tourists from every country in the world

   - ELABORATOR: its underground tunnels for use by employees only

Part Two Directions: Add two of the tools in a good place in the sentence. Copy the sentence and underline the tools you inserted.

On the Mark: Use commas to separate tools from the rest of the sentence.

3. Muhammad Ali appeared on the cover of *Sports Illustrated* thirty-seven times.

   - EXTENDER: because he was the most famous and renowned boxer of all time

   - IDENTIFIER: the only boxer to win the heavyweight championship three times

   - DESCRIBER: making memorable comments such as "float like a butterfly, sting like a bee"

   - ELABORATOR: his style as much dancing as boxing

4. One World Trade Center was erected on the site of the twin towers destroyed in terrorist attacks on September 11, 2001.

   - EXTENDER: after an architect named David Childs was hired to design and build it
   - IDENTIFIER: the tallest building in the Western hemisphere at 1,776 feet
   - DESCRIBER: standing now as the crown jewel of the New York City skyline,
   - ELABORATOR: its presence an important symbol on the New York City skyline

Part Three Directions: Add three of the tools in a good place in the sentence. Copy the sentence and underline the tools you inserted.

On the Mark: Use commas to separate tools from the rest of the sentence.

5. The amazingly popular Harry Potter novels earned multimillions of dollars for first-time novelist J. K. Rowling.

   - EXTENDER: because those stories appealed to readers of all ages everywhere
   - IDENTIFIER: an English author whose fantasy series has sold over 500 million copies worldwide in over seventy languages
   - DESCRIBER: published after a series of rejections by many publishers
   - ELABORATOR: her life forever changed by this success

6. Times Square in New York City attracts millions of tourists annually.

    - EXTENDER: since the area is one the world's greatest entertainment venues

    - IDENTIFIER: the gathering place every December 31 for crowds to welcome the new year when the clock strikes midnight

    - DESCRIBER: entertaining them with Broadway shows, tourist shops, spectacular hotels, and fine restaurants

    - ELABORATOR: its giant neon signs flashing news, entertainment, and advertising

ACTIVITY 2: CREATING TOOLS

Following are sentences about famous people or famous places. You will create tools for your choice of *fifteen* of those sentences. Online or offline, find out interesting information for your tools. Directions follow.

FAMOUS PEOPLE

1. **Elvis Presley** was a hugely popular entertainer but died prematurely from drugs.

2. **Alexander Hamilton** began in total poverty but became the creator of America's financial system.

3. **Steve Jobs** transformed daily life through the invention of many kinds of technology.

4. **Oprah Winfrey** became famous because of her talk show and charitable work.

5. **Rosa Parks** refused to give up her seat to a white person on a bus in Montgomery, Alabama.

6. **Nelson Mandela** was responsible for the end of apartheid in South Africa.

7. **Cleopatra** ruled ancient Egypt and is said to have killed herself with a poisonous snake.

8. **John Kennedy** is among the most popular of American presidents.

9. **Anne Frank** did not survive the concentration camps in World War II, but her journal has become famous.

10. **Henry Ford** invented the first car and the assembly line that made it possible.

FAMOUS PLACES

11. **The Great Wall of China** was built to protect China from the invasion of outsiders.

12. **The Taj Mahal** is an ivory marble structure that was built by the emperor to contain the tomb of his wife.

13. **The Grand Canyon** in the western United States attracts thousands of tourists every summer.

14. **The Pyramids of Giza** include the huge Great Sphinx.

15. **Antarctica** is the coldest, windiest place on earth with icebergs the size of cities and floating ice the size of France.

16. **The luxurious Burj Al Arab Hotel** in Dubai was built on an artificial island to look like a giant sailboat.

17. **Niagara Falls** is where daredevils attempt to go over the gigantic falls in a container without being hurt or killed.

18. **The statues of Easter Island** have mystified modern visitors because of their huge size and location on a tiny island.

19. **Mount Rushmore** in South Dakota contains the carved stone profiles of important American presidents.

20. **The Leaning Tower of Pisa** is a remarkable slanting bell tower.

Part One Directions: Choose any *five* sentences to create and insert one tool. Underline and name each tool in parentheses: *extender*, *identifier*, *describer*, or *elaborator*.

EXAMPLES

No Tools

Napoleon Bonaparte was one of the most famous military leaders in history.

SAMPLES WITH *ONE* TOOL

1. **extender:** Napoleon Bonaparte was one of the most famous military leaders in history, although he wound up alone in exile.

2. **identifier:** Napoleon Bonaparte, a French military and political expert, was one of the most famous military leaders in history.

3. **describer:** Building an empire that included most of Europe, Napoleon Bonaparte was one of the most famous military leaders in history.

    OR

    Studied even today for his military strategies, Napoleon Bonaparte was one of the most famous military leaders in history

4. **elaborator:** Napoleon Bonaparte was one of the most famous military leaders in history, his campaigns studied by others to learn his strategies.

Part Two Directions: Choose *five* other sentences to create and insert *two* tools into your sentences—either two different tools or two of the same kind. Underline and name each tool in parentheses: *extender, identifier, describer,* or *elaborator.*

EXAMPLES

No Tools
The Eiffel Tower in Paris is one of the most famous structures in the world.

SAMPLES WITH TWO *DIFFERENT* TOOLS

1. Constructed over a two-year period for the entrance to the 1889 World's Fair (*describer*), the Eiffel Tower in Paris is one of the most famous structures in the world, its height equal to a building with 81 stories (*elaborator*).

2. Although its appearance at first was criticized as ugly (*extender*), the Eiffel Tower in Paris, the most-visited attraction in that city (*identifier*), is one of the most famous structures in the world.

SAMPLES WITH TWO OF THE *SAME* TOOLS

1. *Two Extenders:* Because it is a very tall climbable structure, the Eiffel Tower in Paris is one of the most famous structures in the world, although today it is not the tallest.

2. *Two Identifiers:* The tallest structure in the city, the Eiffel Tower in Paris is one of the most famous structures in the world, a striking presence visible from anywhere in Paris.

3. *Two Describers:* Climbed by over 7 million people a year, the Eiffel Tower in Paris is one of the most famous structures in the world, rising higher upon its completion than any building in the world.

4. *Two Elaborators:* The Eiffel Tower in Paris, <u>its tremendous height visible from anywhere in the city</u>, is one of the most famous structures in the world, <u>its surface requiring painting every seven years to prevent rusting</u>.

Part Three Directions: Choose *five* more sentences to create and insert *three* tools of any kind into your sentences. <u>Underline</u> and name each tool in parentheses: *extender, identifier, describer,* or *elaborator.*

EXAMPLES

No Tools
Hollywood is the American center for making movies.

SAMPLE WITH *THREE* DIFFERENT TOOLS

The subject of an award-winning film called *La La Land* (*identifier*), Hollywood, <u>situated in the hills of Los Angeles, California</u> (*describer*), is the American center for making movies, <u>its bright lights at movie openings attracting crowds to glimpse movie stars on the red carpet</u> (*elaborator*).

SAMPLE WITH THREE OF THE *SAME* TOOLS

Hollywood, <u>studied by moviemakers worldwide</u> (*describer*), is the American center for making movies, <u>attracting young hopeful actors to its moviemaking machine</u> (*describer*), <u>offering perhaps bright futures and fame</u> (*describer*).

ACTIVITY 3: USING THE TOOLBOX

Directions: This is the last activity. Knock the ball out of the park for a home run. Write *five* strong sentences, pretending they will be published in a book about famous people and places. Here are some ideas for what to write about.

- **FAMOUS PEOPLE**—*entertainers, athletes, inventors, heroes, explorers, authors, villains, monarchs, presidents, or other famous people*
- **FAMOUS PLACES**—*tourist attractions, cities, countries, historic sites, oddities, planets, or other famous places*

Include in each sentence one, two, or three tools in the place of your choice. You choose how many tools to include. Underline and name each tool in parentheses: *extender, identifier, describer,* or *elaborator*. The following chart reviews the tools.

Tool	First Word	Example
EXTENDER	*after, although, as, because, before, if, since, until, when, while*	Marilyn Monroe was known by this Hollywood name, although Elton John used her real name in a song titled "Goodbye, Norma Jean."
IDENTIFIER	*a, an, the*	Baltimore, Maryland, the crab capital of the United States, offers hard crabs from the Chesapeake Bay for great dining.
DESCRIBER	word ending in *-ing* or *-ed*	Picasso invented a new way of painting human figures, shaping them like boxes so the style became called *cubism.* OR Picasso became famous for his painting and sculpture, studied and imitated today by young artists all over the world.

Tool	First Word	Example
ELABORATOR	*my, his, her, its, our, their*	Amsterdam, its streets filled with people riding bicycles, demonstrates another way to travel in cities.

PROCEDURE

Step One: Investigate a person or place to find interesting information.

Step Two: Write a short sentence that begins with the name of the famous person or famous place and then makes an interesting comment about that person or place.

EXAMPLE

Gandhi was the leader of the successful struggle for independence of India from British rule.

Step Three: Add tools in good places—one, two, or three tools of your choice.

EXAMPLES

one tool: Called the Father of the Nation, Gandhi was the leader of the successful struggle for independence of India from British rule. (*Contains one tool—a describer.*)

two tools: Called the Father of the Nation, Gandhi, a firm believer in nonviolent civil disobedience, was the leader of the successful struggle for independence of India from British rule. (*Contains two tools—a describer and an identifier.*)

three tools: Called the Father of the Nation, Gandhi, a firm believer in nonviolent civil disobedience, was the leader of the successful struggle for independence of India from British

rule, an effort that ended in freedom of India from British rule.
(*Contains three tools—a describer and two identifiers.*)

Step Four: Take a bow!

Congratulations! You did it! You stayed focused, stayed the course, and crossed the finish line. You learned that, in composing your sentences, the right tools get the job done right.

In your toolbox you now have powerful sentence-composing tools. You are no longer a sentence novice. Now you are a sentence architect and builder. Use those tools to build strong sentences.

There is nothing more satisfying than having a sentence
fall into place in a way you feel is right, and then
adding another one and then another one.
It's extraordinarily satisfying.

—Yann Martel, author of *Life of Pi*
